FAILING
UP

FAILING UP

UP

HOW TO TAKE RISKS, AIM HIGHER, and NEVER STOP LEARNING

LESLIE ODOM, JR.

FEIWEL AND FRIENDS
New York

A Feiwel and Friends Book
An imprint of Macmillan Publishing Group, LLC
175 Fifth Ave, New York, NY 10010

Our books may be purchased in bulk for promotional, educational,
or business use. Please contact your local bookseller or the Macmillan
Corporate and Premium Sales Department at (800) 221-7945 ext. 5442
or by e-mail at MacmillanSpecialMarkets@macmillan.com.

Library of Congress Control Number: 2017944820

ISBN 978-1-250-13996-2 (hardcover) / ISBN 978-1-250-13997-9 (ebook)

Book design by Raphael Geroni

Feiwel and Friends logo designed by Filomena Tuosto

First edition, 2018

1 3 5 7 9 10 8 6 4 2

fiercereads.com

FOR MY TEACHERS

CONTENTS

TAKE ME TO THE WORLD

> *Take me to the world that's real*
> *Show me how it's done.*

> — STEPHEN SONDHEIM
> from the teleplay *Evening Primrose*

ATE ONE NIGHT IN EARLY 2016, some months before my final performance as Aaron Burr in *Hamilton: An American Musical*, I found myself alone in a darkened Richard Rodgers Theatre. I paused for a moment to take it all in.

For the next week, I would be on a beach in Mexico with my wife, Nicolette. An overdue and much-needed vacation.

After the curtain call, I'd spent a while straightening up my dressing room. I packed a large box with some personal effects. I tried to leave things tidy for the new guy(s). Burr would belong to the understudies in the building for the next week. There were three. And they were ecstatic. Who could blame them? It was the role of a lifetime, and for the following seven days, it was all theirs.

My tiny dressing room had slowly accumulated piles of workout clothes, extra pairs of shoes, books, snacks, drawings, letters, and small gifts from fans. It was my home away from home. I did my best to thin it out in there. The new Burrs deserved a clean slate.

Angelo, the late-night doorman at the Rodgers, had just bounced.

"Les, stay as long as you want," he told me. "When you leave, make sure you don't forget anything. The door will lock behind you."

The Cancun flight was early in the a.m., but before I took off, I made a sharp right outside my dressing room, and followed the familiar path to the stage entrance.

I'd never been completely alone in the theater before.

Looking out at the empty seats, I took a mental snapshot—doing my best not to forget anything.

For two years *Hamilton* had been such an enormous part of my life. The changes in the wake of the Broadway opening had been so seismic that sometimes there were nights like this one when I would spend a few moments trying to piece together . . . understand . . . *how*?

Hamilton was the dream that almost didn't happen. Only five years prior to encountering Lin-Manuel Miranda's masterpiece, I had made the decision to move on from the business of being an actor.

HAMILTON was the DREAM that ALMOST DIDN'T HAPPEN.

I found myself at one of life's most common rites of passage, a *graduation*, and I knew from past experience that there would be things I'd have to leave behind. Some things don't travel well from one time in your life to the next. Like broken-down rides and ratty furniture—bad habits, toxic relationships, unhealthy thought patterns—there should be shedding around graduation day. The old stuff will only weigh you down.

On the threshold of a milestone birthday, I questioned whether I needed to lighten up.

Graduating into my thirties felt significant. The

instability and unpredictability of the artist's path was starting to feel like a child's way to live. Things may have been intensified by another rite of passage that I knew little about at the time. There's a cosmic correlation that happens around the age of twenty-nine known to astrologers as the Saturn Return.

The slow-moving planet Saturn takes twenty-nine and a half years to complete its orbit around the sun and return to the exact same spot in the sky as it was on the day you were born.

The Saturn Return is notoriously disruptive—known for upheaval and thrusting things taken for granted into question. Whether or not you believe in those influences (and I take it all with a few grains of salt) it makes sense that whenever you hit that natural cusp between your extended younger years and adulthood, you can expect uncertainty and apprehension with the onrush of big change.

I was taking stock of where I was at twenty-nine and seriously pondering the real possibility that if I didn't make some different choices, who's to say I wouldn't be in the exact same spot at *thirty*-nine? My chosen path offered so few assurances. Who's to say I wouldn't be in the exact same spot at *FORTY*-nine? Life on fast-forward had me circling the drain. Some paradigm-shifting advice from a mentor and practical application brought me from one of the saddest times in my life to a Broadway stage at (what felt like) the center of the theatrical universe for a time and . . . wait—*what time is it?*

Cancun. (!!!)

I stepped out of the Richard Rodgers Theatre and into the frigid New York City night air. The stage door dumps you into the alley behind the theater.

The big metal door slammed and locked behind me as my buddy Angelo promised.

A preview.

There was another graduation looming.

Only six months left of *Hamilton* on Broadway for me. There had been so much hard work to get here, and it was already halfway over.

You can't stay any one place forever. Box of personal effects in hand, I kept walking.

My apartment was a short fifteen-minute walk from work. It was along the trek that night that the first principles for the conversation at the heart of this book came to mind.

In part to keep warm, I got my legs moving as fast as my thoughts were that night.

I've had a profound appreciation for the role of the mentor since elementary school. My fifth-grade social studies teacher was the first. As a kid with some behavioral issues, my story would've unfolded in a drastically different way without people who cared. I've included some of the greatest lessons I've learned at their instruction in the pages of this book.

Among the mentors was—and is—a Los Angeles acting/life/empowerment coach, expert Boggle champ, and Renaissance man named Stuart K Robinson, a brilliant guy whose practical wisdom has changed many lives. And I swear I'd say the same thing even if he *hadn't* let me marry his daughter.

In the throes of my Saturn Return crisis, I asked Stu if he had any time to talk. He'd helped people through career transitions before.

We met for food, and after listening thoughtfully to all the reasons why I had decided to leave the business (sick of this, tired of that, regular depression, tokenism, student loans, no money, *add complaint here*), Stuart paused for a moment to make sure I was prepared to hear him.

I sat up in my seat. Ready to listen.

He began, "Les, of course you can quit. That's fine. And we can talk about what you might do next and how to go about it. I can support you in that. But I'd love to see you *try* before you quit."

"BUT I'D LOVE to SEE YOU *TRY* BEFORE YOU QUIT."

Try? What did he mean, *try?*

As a working actor for over a decade, I had the wounds, calluses, and IMDb credits to show for it. When an opportunity presented itself you'd be hard-pressed to find many people who tried harder. Stuart knew this and still he was looking at me and telling me he wanted me to try?

He said, "You know how to succeed when the phone is ringing. But what about when the phone's *not* ringing?"

Stu went on, "What did you do for *yourself* today? Did you call anyone? In what ways did you take charge of your creative life today? Did you send an e-mail to someone who might be working on something you care about? Did you read anything? Did you write anything? Did you take a class? Did you practice? What step forward did you take for yourself today in the absence of the ringing phone?"

The solution was so simple and it had completely eluded me. Stu was reminding me of that thing we all know deep down: if you are willing to take one meaningful step on your own behalf toward making a dream come true today, the Universe will meet you where you are and help you take *two*. The Universe will never shortchange you. When you take steps to better yourself it is never in vain.

Make no mistake, following your dream has a spiritual component as well.

You will train and prepare to actualize your dreams in countless ways. Try not to neglect spiritual fortification. For some, it's a vulnerability point they don't realize until the need becomes dire.

Stu's advice led me back to class; it led to a more consistent ratio of bookings when the phone was ringing; it led to a focus on music, live performing, and independent work when the phone was not ringing; it led me in a direct and traceable line all the way to *Hamilton* and the most creatively fulfilling, educational time of my life. It continues to this day.

There was failure before. After, too. In drafting these pages, I try to choose personal stories and life lessons to help illustrate my thesis that *spectacular failure* is the secret ingredient to your ultimate success.

You will learn and grow from the former at a rate far greater than the latter.

Almost home now.

Lin-Manuel Miranda stalked an impulse—an inspiration—for *six years*. He is, among many things, a master editor as well as a monster with the pen. Lin's a guy who can tell you about failure. He'll write you a song about it and that song will make you weep. And once the world was introduced to his passion and craftsmanship, he's a guy who can tell you all about success, too.

He picked up Ron Chernow's biography about a complicated historical figure and wrote an entire musical odyssey that begins with the question: *How . . . ?*

He tracks the founding of a nation in the three-hour roller-coaster ride that follows, as he pulls pieces together to discover *how* a "bastard, orphan, son of a whore" born in squalor, in a "forgotten spot in the Caribbean" grows up to be "a hero and a scholar."

I love questions that begin with *how*. They activate the listener. You become a historian or a detective—piecing together your findings and following your intuition on the way to your response.

We learn from the pages of history who we are and who we have been. We learn from our greatness and our darkness. We cannot predict the future, but studying where we've been helps us better understand where we are.

We learn *how* we can do better.

Predictions are overrated. On the *Hamilton* stage alone, looking out at the empty seats—no one could've predicted the place where we'd find ourselves from the place where we began.

And while no one can predict *exactly* where your ingenuity, your perseverance, and your willingness to fail spectacularly will lead you . . . the smart money is on UP.

Go get it.

The game's afoot. And the game is good.

CHAPTER 1

THE MENTOR

> *When a man starts out to build a world,*
> *he starts first with himself.*
>
> —LANGSTON HUGHES

> *The delicate balance of mentoring someone is not*
> *creating them in your own image, but giving them the*
> *opportunity to create themselves.*
>
> —STEVEN SPIELBERG

 OW?

How do you figure out what it is that you're really meant to do in this life? How do you find your point of entry? How do you begin?

A few people I've met seem to have been born to their calling, with gifts and dreams that stood out early on. Most of us don't fall into that category. Most of us have no idea at the start what we're meant to do or even what we're capable of. Some of us don't find *our thing* so much as it finds us. And sometimes it's only because of some special person who introduces us to possibilities we might never have imagined for ourselves.

Like many others, I have an early educator to thank for helping me make that initial connection. Mrs. Frances Turner was my fifth-grade social studies teacher and my very first mentor.

I was a rowdy, unfocused ten-year-old when I arrived in her classroom, and I can't say we hit it off right away.

Back then, I couldn't think of a subject more dry and joyless than social studies, and I held Mrs. Turner in contempt for having voluntarily chosen it at some point as the subject she would teach. What kind of a person would *choose* social studies?

Mrs. Turner never smiled. She was all business and immune to my limited charms.

What bothered me most, Frances seemed to understand me in a way that was unsettling.

I WAS a HANDFUL.

I was a handful. That had been the case since kindergarten back in New York, where I spent the first seven years of my life.

In my kindergarden classroom, we had what was known as the "Sad-Face Box." It looked very much like the name suggests. It was a box drawn each day in the bottom left corner of the blackboard. At the top of the box, Ms. Lewis drew . . . well, a "sad face."

Looked kinda like the emoji ☹.

Names of the students who broke rules would go into the box. She kept a running tally of naughty kids and mine was, without fail, the very first name in that stupid box every single day. Half the time it would be so early in the day that she hadn't even gotten around to drawing the thing yet when I'd give her a reason to reach for her chalk.

I'd purposely speed through an assignment so she'd be faced with the hassle of finding me something else to do, or I would crack a joke that only my section of the room could hear and get a bunch of toddlers riled up.

Ms. Lewis would draw that Sad Face and put a box around it in a fit of rage. She'd break the chalk pressing too hard as she spelled out my name. You could feel her wishing it had more letters or that she could add punctuation after it, she'd be so pissed off.

L-E-S-L-I-E.!.!!!!!.!~!*###??!!!!=+&&@

Children who were well behaved for the remainder of the day would find their names erased from the box as easily as they had been written.

In a particularly nice touch from Ms. Lewis, before the end of each day, she would find a way to erase *all* the names still left inside the Sad-Face Box. If, for a full minute, you could manage to sit with your hands folded, your back straight, and your mouth "zipped," if you could find some discipline and self-control for the final *minute* of the day, you'd start the following day with a clean slate. A kindergarten teacher's lesson in redemption was also baked into the Box.

Still, I didn't have the tools yet to understand how to make myself behave like the other kids. I had no clue how to begin to put my energy to better use. It would take five more years and the help of a no-nonsense social studies teacher to help me figure that out.

AS I GOT OLDER, I REALIZED THAT PART OF my problem was the fact that I was one of those kids who felt (to himself anyway) like an adult on the inside.

When I turned thirty, I thought: *Yeah, this is the age I've felt like since I was eight.* Maybe even younger.

As a kid, I had trouble with rules and unquestioned authority. My mouth got me into a fair amount of trouble. I wanted to know *why* I was being asked to do a particular thing before I was going to do it.

"Put your heads down!"

Hand raised and question posed in a polite but thinly veiled accusatory tone: "Why?"

"If you finish your quiz before the bell, use the extra time to check your work. And no talking."

In a tone laced with suspicion and distrust: "Why?"

Today I understand that in classrooms filled with more than thirty other students, my teachers didn't have the seconds or the engery to take my earnest but ill-timed questions to heart. Back then, I wanted my concerns to be on the record.

Mom and Dad were fairly strict. If I found myself in some sort of trouble at school, I knew my transgressions would always have to be *defensible*. There would have to be a gray area that I could highlight. There would have to be Their Side, and My Side. When I pleaded my case at home there needed to be nuance and perspective. Or my goose would be cooked.

My parents would always hear me out. They would never ever take a teacher's word or anyone's word completely over mine.

That was the law, never to be changed. Until one day in the fall of 1991 when Frances Turner summoned my father for a parent-teacher conference one morning before school.

Monday through Friday, Leslie Odom, Sr., was wound tight, tight, tight. He had the shortest fuse of anyone I knew. Dad worked in sales. He spent the bulk of our childhood years (my baby sister, Elizabeth, came along when I was six) climbing the ladder in corporate America, and while he rarely let the world know it, the pressure took a toll.

Mom was Dad's partner in upward mobility. She worked in the field of recreation and rehabilitation therapy for as long as I can remember. Her pure goodness and capacity for empathy never ceased to amaze me.

Yevette Marie Nixon filled my world with light. Always slow to anger where I was concerned, she was my first teacher. She taught me to add and subtract, she read to me, and eventually she taught me to read to myself. My little sister takes after Mom, too. Sweet as can be.

With two educated, working parents, I understood their expectation of me extremely well very early on.

Dad's position was straightforward: "The same way I go to work every day and your mother goes to work every day, that's what we expect from you. School is your job. No excuses."

If I was falling down on *my* job and it made it harder for him to do *his* job . . . it wasn't just the anger and discipline to be meted out later that twisted my stomach in knots, it was also the fact that I was letting down the whole family unit.

But I simply couldn't get it together in school. I was a prideful, mouthy kid (with a bit of a short fuse myself), who couldn't resist the urge to make it known if an adult was being hypocritical or arbitrary. My mini-crusades were almost always about some injustice.

AS I SAT IN THE FRONT SEAT OF THE CAR
with my dad, driving to this meeting with Mrs. Turner, I
had no way of gauging what he would think of her. Today
I have a better sense of how formidable she must have
been in person.

Frances Turner was brilliant, elegant, and econom-
ical in life and in her style as an educator. Frances was
distinguished among her peers, and I always felt that
she carried herself more like a tenured college professor
than a fifth-grade social studies teacher. Well-read and
well-traveled, Fran rocked a short, cropped Afro and one-
of-a-kind frocks she picked up on outings to the Kenyan
marketplace. There was a dignity and regality in everything
she did. It came from a clear understanding of her place
in the world and of her personal power within it. She was
charged with shaping minds.

While it's true that in the first couple of weeks in her
classroom I never saw her laugh, I never saw her scream,
either. She wouldn't have wasted even a bead of sweat on a
behavioral issue. Not at Masterman, one of Philadelphia's
prestigious and elite "magnet" schools, which required
testing and interviews to attend. Her attitude implied that

if you were fortunate enough to be here, you would respect the privilege.

Mrs. Turner ushered my father into a closed-door meeting in her classroom that morning. I waited in the hallway.

The meeting extended on and on. Dad was in there forever.

I could not see this ending well for me.

When he emerged from the classroom twenty minutes later, nothing in his face gave me any hint whatsoever as to what the lady had said to him. "Enjoy your day. See you at home," he said. And then he was off.

The tense good-bye told me all I needed to know about what would eventually happen when I saw my father at home that night. I spent the day working on My Side.

IT WAS ONE of the LONGEST SCHOOL DAYS that I CAN REMEMBER.

It was one of the longest school days that I can remember.

That night, Dad came home from work, and there was still no mention of the meeting. Dinnertime came. I dragged myself to the table, where the conversation was muted.

When my father finally spoke, I was expecting his rage. Instead, he was measured.

"I have never ever taken somebody's word without hearing your side first. I have never done that."

I waited for what was coming.

"With Mrs. Turner, I will take her word. With Mrs. Turner, you don't have a side."

The law had changed. I was on notice.

"If you misbehave in her classroom or if you ever disrespect her again, you're going to have a real problem with me." That was his final word on the matter.

Dad had given Frances all the power.

I let it sink in.

Dad has always been tough on me—though my behavioral issues in school were tough on *him*. My folks were only a little older than children when they started a family and began having children themselves. I believe he really was doing his best. I believed it then, too.

At the end of the day, I trusted my dad. And if he trusted Mrs. Turner, it meant that I could, too.

·

TRUST OPENED THE DOOR TO ONE OF THE most formative and valuable relationships of my young life.

The tension and hostility faded away. Frances and I became congenial, even friendly, over the time after her meeting with my dad. I began to regard Mrs. Turner as someone in whom I could confide.

TRUST OPENED the DOOR TO ONE of the MOST FORMATIVE and VALUABLE RELATIONSHIPS of MY YOUNG LIFE.

Trust meant that when Mrs. Turner told me I should enter the citywide African-American Oratorical Competition because she felt I had a real shot at being a contender, I would take heed and get to work.

Having a platform to speak my mind was unheard of. Like most ten-year-olds, I'd been told that I was supposed to be seen and not heard. Now I was being encouraged to take a stand and speak truth to power in front of a room of adults.

Kids from all over Philadelphia wrote and delivered original speeches. The orations were judged on content and delivery. Prizes and trophies went to top scorers, but the greatest reward was seeing my potential in a new light.

It's impossible for me to overstate the effect that oratory and the competition had on me as a young person.

With patience and diligence and grace, Mrs. Turner led me to the writer, and in many ways, the warrior within me. Every kid needs an outlet, a world in which they can discover and see themselves at their best.

That first year that I entered the competition, my best wasn't quite good enough to win the grand prize. I came in second but vowed I would be back the following year to try again. I failed to come in first, but I loved the process so much, I used my near miss as motivational fuel.

When I hear people complain or bemoan coming close to a sought-after goal and missing by inches, I am quick to reassure them. Celebrate the fight and the proud run. Coming close can be confirmation you are on the right path. What can you do better the next time? What can you do to make yourself more prepared for the next time?

Mrs. Turner was just as motivated. We went back to the drawing board. We retooled and reentered the following year.

EVERY KID NEEDS an OUTLET,
A WORLD in which THEY CAN DISCOVER
and SEE THEMSELVES at THEIR BEST.

For the next four years—the rest of my time in middle school and even my first year of high school—my coach and I went undefeated in the Philadelphia competition. We had quite a run.

Our winnings included thousands of dollars in savings bonds (which went directly to my college tuition in my first year), two brand-new Apple desktop computers with printers (the very first computers my family owned), and a scholarship to begin studying drama (my first formal training of any kind) at Philadelphia's Freedom Theatre, one of the oldest and most prestigious African-American repertory companies in the country.

Located on Broad and Master streets in North Philadelphia, the Freedom Theatre was a rose growing out of the concrete. Inside the walls of Freedom was an oasis of learning and empowerment.

Each student who entered the theater was greeted by Thom Page, the director of the training program. Page acted as threshold guardian, a job he took as seriously as a heart attack.

You had to know the password to get past Mr. Page. It sent the message right away that inside these walls, there was something worthy of protection.

"What's the password?" Mr. Page would ask.

"I respect myself!" you would offer.

"You're beautiful!" was always Thom's reply.

To every single child who walked in. Every single day.

Maybe I would have found my way to Freedom Theatre and to my eventual path without the guidance of Frances Turner. But I can't be sure.

Oratory was the gateway to the theater and Mrs. Turner helped me discover the password. She reframed notions that I was bound for trouble. She freed my voice and gave it back to me with style.

Mrs. Turner was a vessel for small miracles.

On the way UP, there's plenty you can do on your own. There's a great deal in these pages about how to make the best use of an hour of private time. The work you put in when no one is watching will matter far more than the work you do when the cameras are rolling. The private hours of hard work you dedicate in the dark will be their own testament when you're finally standing in your light.

You can do a lot on your own. But no one can do it *all* alone.

Who is your Frances Turner?

Even if you aren't exactly where you'd like to be, I'm willing to bet you have a host of people to thank for the best parts of your journey so far. There's a mentor, there's a teacher, there's a friend who believed in you. Let's make your rise to the top the way you say thank you to the person who helped you see your own magnificent potential.

You've more than likely encountered bullies and naysayers on the path as well. There will always be people around us who are invested in proving their skepticism right. Make this the moment you wrestle your life back from the hands of bullies and the tormentors of your past and the ones you'll face tomorrow.

This is your time.

We owe it to our mentors and we owe it to ourselves.

Onward.

CHAPTER 2

THE BIG
BREAK

Be more than ready. . . . Start now, every day, becoming,
in your actions, your regular actions, what you would
like to become in the bigger scheme of things.

— ANNA DEAVERE SMITH

 **DIDN'T WANT TO BE IN SHOW** business. I wanted to be in *Rent.*

I was sixteen years old and I had never been to see a Broadway show, but I wanted to be in *Rent* on Broadway more than anything.

Broadway was expensive. The best seats in the house could run upward of seventy-five dollars a ticket! It's somewhat laughable today but then, it was too steep for our middle-class family of four.

I didn't know anyone in show business. And for a long time, I don't think it even registered for me that these were jobs you could seek out.

Twenty years before *Hamilton*, *Rent* was also a far-reaching phenomenon with a hardworking team behind it doing their due diligence to ensure it was making noise on the national stage as well as in New York. I remember seeing the cover of *Newsweek* with Adam Pascal and Daphne Rubin-Vega on newsstands. I remember watching a TV news magazine feature that gave us a glimpse inside what was happening at the Nederlander Theatre on Broadway eight times a week.

The next day, I went to the record store to sample the cast album.

THE NEXT DAY, I WENT to the RECORD STORE to SAMPLE the CAST ALBUM.

I'd meant to only listen to a song or two. Ninety minutes later I was still standing there. Frozen. I was at the cash register five minutes after that ponying up the $19.99 for my very own copy of the double-disk recording—more than I'd ever spent on a single piece of art.

For a long list of reasons, *Rent* was a revelation to me. I wanted to be friends with these people. I wanted to dress how they dressed and eat what they ate. I wanted to love how they loved. My heart took residence in the world Jonathan Larson created. The themes and motifs spoke to me like the gospels. Friendship in the face of death. Love in the face of death. Art in the face of capitalism and consumerism. Protest in the face of injustice.

This was my tribe.

Jonathan Larson composed a tuneful and emotional Broadway score fashioned in modern rock and pop music. It sounded like music you'd hear on contemporary radio. It's a very hard feat in the theater. It requires a unique talent. It requires someone who possesses skills as both classic storyteller *and* hit songwriter. It happens rarely, but when it does, the results can be magic.

I knew every note and syllable of the score in a few weeks' time.

A dream started for me here.

I began to believe somewhere inside myself that I could *will* my way into the world that had captured my imagination.

Star or roadie, usher or ensemble member—I didn't know what the capacity would be. But I believed that there could be, *in* or *around* the thing that I loved, a place with my name on it.

And there is no wasted time in the company of something or someone that you love.

Learning the songs, reading whatever I could get my hands on about the show and its humble beginnings at New York Theatre Workshop, soaking up the stories about Jonathan and the young cast of performers getting their big breaks standing at the center of the phenomenon, it was all preparation for the far-off time when I would find myself immersed in that world. Though if someone would've told me how soon that immersion would arrive, I wouldn't have believed them.

Nothing can stop you from preparing for your dream opportunity. But you can't know the day or the hour it will come to you.

You walk toward the things that make you feel most alive. You walk toward the things you love. You love them with your whole heart. Read about them. Talk about them. Find other people who love those things, too. And eventually, the thing you love most in the world will love you back. It is inevitable. Not always in the way you expect, but in exactly the way you need. The loving energy you put toward your dreams is magnified and returned to you in time.

I WAS VERY LUCKY TO COME OF AGE IN Philadelphia at the time that I did, and I'm sure I didn't know it.

Looking back to when and where my dream first took form, I realize I was a part of a whole group of young people who were on a similar path. Friends from my childhood went on to achieve great things in their chosen creative fields.

America's fifth largest city, Philly is marked by a reverence for history, education, and the arts.

Your hometown will shape your taste and your developing eye. Most of us travel a far distance from home in pursuit of the things we love most. But for better or worse, you take your hometown with you. Your hometown is the salt in the stew. Philadelphia is a huge part of *who* and *why* I am.

It was at the Merriam Theater on Philadelphia's Avenue of the Arts where I first saw the touring production of *Rent*. The tour was in town for six weeks. I got a twenty-dollar student rush ticket and took in the show from the front row.

The lights went down and my heart beat a little faster in my chest.

I spent act one with a big, fat grin plastered on my face. The whole thing played like one continuous favorite song. When intermission came, my cheeks hurt from smiling and my head was swimming with the images I'd just witnessed. The show was perfect. Even better than what I'd imagined after listening to the songs hundreds of times.

Act two began and a small, seemingly insignificant, improvised moment between two actors on the stage—a flash of connection—burned into my memory banks and opened a brand-new door in the annexes of my imagination.

FROM MY FRONT-ROW SEAT, I CLOCK AN actor as he enters from stage right. He is wearing the most genuine and warm smile you can picture. There is a secret behind his eyes. He winks at a woman across the stage from him. It is quick and subtle, and if I wasn't in the front row, there was no way I would've noticed it. A similar smile creeps across the woman's face. She has a secret, too. They take their places among the rest of the cast with their smiles and secrets intact. They sing about seasons of love and the remainder of act two unfolds from there.

"Five hundred twenty-five thousand six hundred minutes . . ."

I am not certain anyone else noticed the wink or if it would have meant anything to them if they had. It was such a small thing, but at the risk of hyperbole, it was one of the greatest moments of my entire life, and I was never the same again ever!

THE WINK GAVE ME the TINIEST GLIMPSE into the LIFE that CONTINUED to UNFOLD OFFSTAGE.

Too much? Okay, that may be overstating it a bit, but I'll tell you why it mattered to me for real. After so many listens to the album and imagining what the show might look like, I'd spent the entire first act utterly enrapt by what was unfolding onstage. The wink gave me the tiniest glimpse into the life that continued to unfold *off*stage.

Life continued in the wings and in the dressing rooms. There were probably genuine friendships, embraces, inside jokes, private moments that we were witnessing the whole time and didn't even realize. They were incorporating it all into the show. Life and art, then, were intrinsic and even interchangeable.

Boundaries could be erased between the two and the result was a richer and more deeply felt experience. Life was happening before they entered the stage and it didn't stop once they made their exits. This wasn't a museum piece. It was not fixed in time. It was a living, breathing thing, susceptible to change as subtle as a wink.

The theater became a 4-D experience for me in that moment. The cost of my ticket had been twenty dollars, but there was no dollar amount you could place on the experience I had that afternoon. Afterward, I no longer dreamed solely of the day I would become a cast member in my favorite Broadway show. I dreamed of a life where the art didn't stop just because I'd left the stage.

LIFE CAN TURN ON A DIME.

At the end of my junior year of high school, a few months before my seventeenth birthday, I spent hours in line for my chance to be heard. *Rent* was holding an open call in my city at a nightclub on 8th Street called Shampoo.

Standing in that line, which wrapped around the block, I was confident of only one thing: no one would be able to say that they loved this work of art more totally or purely than I. My preparation had made me fearless, and I had no expectations.

There's *nothing* like preparation to make you fearless.

As far as prep work was concerned, there was all the time I had spent over years walking toward the thing I loved, and there was the Freedom Theatre.

Freedom Theatre had been a cradle and training ground. I came to it with no knowledge, no experience other than singing in church, and a certain confidence that came from public speaking. As I had a chance to observe the advanced students, who were so polished, I saw a way that I could ascend as they had and make myself proud.

There weren't a lot of politics or favoritism at Freedom. As a student, you rose in the ranks based on your merits. Anyone who was in the advanced class was there because they had earned it. Many of the students had been studying since they were four and five years old. I had a lot of catching up to do.

The discipline appealed to me. I was up for the challenge. I loved the fun and the silliness of performing most of all. The *art* of being silly is vastly underrated in my opinion. I was hooked on the joy.

By the time I was in high school, I sought further training. The Philadelphia Dance Company (Philadanco) in West Philadelphia has a long track record and an esteemed reputation for its rigorous and thorough training of black dancers. Philadanco was founded by Joan Myers Brown, a talented and driven black ballerina and native Philadelphian. Growing up, she saw firsthand the limited professional and educational resources for black dancers in the city, especially when it came to the classical arts. Joan responded by starting her own professional modern dance company and world-class training program. Today, Philadanco is one of the most venerable professional dance companies in the country, and its training program is second to none. It is a rigorous, varied, and serious program for serious dancers.

I was the worst in the class. By far.

I say it with a smile but I mean it completely. Being the worst is a gift in your training. I've pulled up the rear more times than I can count. If you can help it, you want to study in close proximity to people whom you feel you can learn from. There's no place better to be, in a dance class anyway, than on your toes.

I loved the rigors of my early ballet classes and the incremental improvements I was able to see in myself from week to week. It kept me inspired and hungry.

Lessons learned in that West Philadelphia dance studio are with me always. My early dance teachers taught us a head-to-toe body awareness and gave us a world-class technical foundation. If you could cut it at Danco, you could cut it anywhere.

The hours and hours of preparation at Philadanco and Freedom gave me the confidence that I could be a contender as I stood in the line in front of Shampoo, waiting for my audition number.

We all have our own versions of auditions, right? Tests and tryouts at school, interviews for colleges and jobs. There's a scrutiny we face whenever we choose to pursue an opportunity we desire. Nerves creep in and threaten your ability to do your best. Pressure and nerves are real, but they don't have to be crippling. The difference in how you fare can sometimes come down to where you place your focus. You can focus on how much you hate the feeling of being judged or you can focus on appreciation and gratitude for the fact that every audition brings you closer to the place you desire to be.

Every no you'll hear is a no on the way to your ultimate yes. You don't have a thing to be afraid of.

EVERY NO YOU'LL HEAR IS a NO on the WAY to YOUR ULTIMATE YES.

The *Rent* audition was just about the most fun I could imagine. It's exhilarating to be that close to something you've dreamt about. I sang my favorite song in the world for the casting directors, the Donny Hathaway arrangement of "For All We Know."

There might not be a more inappropriate song I could've chosen as audition material, but I had no idea.

It wasn't "pop" and it certainly wasn't "rock," both of which were what they asked for, but my love and exuberance spoke well for me, and I got a callback for later that afternoon.

They gave me a cassette tape and sheet music for a handful of songs they wanted me to be prepared to perform when I returned. I sailed through the new tunes at the callback as if I'd been practicing them for years.

Because I *had* been practicing them for years.

The initial audition in Philadelphia was in the spring, just weeks before the start of summer vacation. Over the next few months the casting office requested my presence in New York three times for different phases of the audition process. I sort of thought, *They must have a database of hundreds of hopefuls from around the country. If I do really well, they'll put me in that database. Maybe a few years from now, a slot will open up and I'll get my chance!*

It was big local news when R & B singer Jill Scott was cast in the Canadian tour of *Rent*. Jill had waited in line with me at Shampoo for her chance to be seen as well.

She was already a major superstar in our home-town. The city celebrated with her when her number was called and she was given the chance to shine on a bigger stage.

My number was called just a short time later.

It was eleven a.m. on a Monday morning, and I was on my way out the door for my summer job at the local NAACP, where I got paid to answer phones, take messages, open and sort through mail and whatnot.

The phone rang and I had a funny feeling. It sounded different to me.

"Hello?"

"Hello, may I please speak to Leslie Odom, Jr.?" a cheery voice on the other end inquired.

"This is Leslie."

"Hi, Leslie! This is Brig Berney, calling from the company management office of the Broadway and touring companies of *Rent*. How are you?"

"I'm fine."

"Good! Well, all of us over here were just crazy about your last audition, and we would love to offer you a spot in our Broadway company. What do you think? The position would start immediately."

I couldn't believe it. "Are you serious?"

"I am very serious," Brig said with a smile in his voice.

Brig has since become a friend of mine. He's still one of the kindest people you'll meet in the big city. He's told me that, at the time, making these calls, giving people their first opportunities to walk onto a Broadway stage, being the first to deliver the news to someone that their dream was coming true, was his favorite part of the job.

"We're sending you a train ticket." Brig said.

"Okay, but you don't have to do that," I told him. "My parents will say yes, but I have to ask them first. They'll drive me."

I had just been invited to join the Broadway company of *Rent* for exactly one month. It was two weeks after my seventeenth birthday and the end of summer 1998.

Arrangements were made for me to take a leave of absence from school. My parents drove me to New York the very next day. I picked up my script, got a dressing room assignment, and had my first blocking rehearsal onstage at the Nederlander Theatre on Broadway.

In twenty-four hours, my summer job had gotten a major upgrade.

MY PERSONAL FEELING ABOUT THE LUCK of the beginner is that it has a lot to do with the absence of cynicism.

Beginners are too filled with optimism for cynicism to dim their light. They are too filled with joy for jadedness to dampen their enthusiasm. This magnetizes the beginner. And it isn't about youth. It is about freshness, and openness, and love. Who wouldn't want to be around that? Every now and then it is the job of the veteran to reconnect with the beginner inside.

As an adult, once you enter the real world, your lack of cynicism can go by the wayside quicker than you think. Once your dream is tied to how you pay your rent and put food on the table, it's easy to forget the joy you felt at the outset.

When your dream shows up, I hope you'll make a commitment to yourself to meet it with as much childhood joy and wonder as possible.

MY CONTRACT WAS EXTENDED TWICE.
The guy I was temporarily replacing was out on injury and each time his doctor suggested he take a little more time, my dream was extended for four more weeks. Ultimately, I got to hang out in the building for three months.

Onstage, as you can imagine, I was in heaven. The heavy lifting had been done long before I suited up and stepped onto the stage at the Nederlander. By the time I'd arrived, the show had been open for three years. It was a Tony- and Pulitzer-award winner and runaway success at the box office. It was one of the most coveted jobs on Broadway. The audience was filled with people who loved the show as much as we did. Everyone in the cast knew how lucky we were to be a small part of giving away this phenomenon each night.

The themes of the piece, woven with great care by creator and composer Jonathan Larson, were made painfully resonant by his sudden and untimely death on the eve of *Rent*'s first off-Broadway preview. There was a reverence and a responsibility we carried with us when we stepped onto that stage. You would've had to be thickheaded and insensitive to miss the vibe. It was in the wood. The feeling was in the scaffolding. The show always connected with people. It always worked. All you had to do was play your position, hold up your little end and the evening would soar.

———◆———

THE NIGHT OF MY FIRST PERFORMANCE, Tina Oh, the show's dance captain, offered to take me for a quick bite before the eight o'clock curtain. Tina had spent the week getting me up to speed. As a replacement in a Broadway show, you get a week to learn your part and then you're on.

Tina took me to a bistro on the corner of 41st and 8th. We talked about our hometowns and our training. She told me all about when she moved to New York. She filled me in on her career as a professional ballet dancer. I'd spent the week learning from Tina during the days and then watching her laser-sharp, exquisite execution of the show at night. I was a big fan. Tina was in her midtwenties, as was most of the cast. I'd had a hard time connecting with people during that first week. It's no wonder. I may have felt like a grown-up on the inside, but I was still very much a kid. I couldn't drink. I couldn't get into bars or clubs. No one had much interest in hanging out at the soda shop with the high school senior.

An hour or so into our meal, Tina told me she had a gift for me. She pulled out something wrapped in tissue paper, and there was a card attached. Even before opening anything, her kindness had rendered me speechless.

The card read: *Dear Leslie, Congratulations! Take a deep breath tonight and a snapshot of this moment in your mind. A Broadway debut only happens once. Break a leg. You're going to be wonderful.*

Inside the tissue paper was a leather-bound journal.

A deep gratitude lodged in the center of my chest. I was full in a way that I hadn't yet experienced in my young life. That night, I made my Broadway debut.

Rent begins with the entire company making their entrance together. For about thirty seconds after that, the audience would routinely go nuts. I'd watched the same reaction for a week at this point. Tonight was no different, except for the fact that on this night, *I* was among the lucky ones who got to be on the receiving end of all that energy.

I took my place onstage alongside the rest of the company and looked out at an audience already going wild.

I thanked God. I took my mental snapshot and a very deep breath. I smiled. And I winked at Tina.

FROM THEN ON, THIS WOULD BE THE BAR against which I would measure all other creative experiences. Does it feel as good as that felt? Do I feel the same sense of fulfillment as I felt during that time?

Rent was artistically fulfilling, culturally relevant, and commercially successful. It doesn't get any better than that in the world of entertainment, and it doesn't come around that often. It would be fifteen years or so until I found my way into a piece of work that would hit all those notes again.

The interim years were filled with effort, some success, plenty of failure, and faith. Faith will deliver the reminder that disappointment and failure don't have to be fatal. In those times when you have done your very best and still come up short, faith fills in the gaps between your reality and your dreams. Faith is what sustains you in the wilderness.

FAITH is WHAT SUSTAINS YOU in the WILDERNESS.

For three months, I was treated like a professional actor. I joined the union. I paid taxes and put money away for retirement. At the stage door, I signed *Rent* tickets and programs and took Polaroids with fans. It was a huge leap forward for me and a dream realized. It would be hard to argue with someone who might call that my Big Break.

You hear a lot about the Big Break from successful people. But I would challenge you to think of your Big Break as an *inside job* instead of something that you'll find externally. The external world will eventually *mirror* what you begin on the inside of yourself today.

When I got back home to Philadelphia, I was committed

to whatever hard work it was going to take to make sure I saw a Broadway stage once more.

The biggest break is the one you will give yourself by choosing to believe in your vision, in what you love, and in the gifts you have to offer the waiting world.

CHAPTER 3

WHAT YOU OWN

 **LEFT** *RENT* **RIGHT BEFORE THE** holidays in '98. Back to Philly. I hated to admit it, but I was run-down and in serious need of a break. By my final curtain call, I was just a few days ahead of a nasty flu that would knock me completley out of commission for a couple weeks. None of this should have surprised anyone. It takes time to build up the stamina to do eight shows a week on Broadway. I'd gone from crawling to walking so quickly.

When I was hired initially, I was given a four-week contract. Prior to that, the longest run of a show that I had done was maybe four performances. Total. I was used to school plays and community theater. Some shows opened and closed within the same weekend. So, from the start, the prospect of getting to do *Rent* thirty-two times on a Broadway stage was almost too good to be true. When one month turned into three months, the physical toll of almost a hundred shows was significant.

Rent is a notoriously challenging score. The show was many singers' first professional job in the theater. Sadly, for some, it would be their last. Without solid vocal training, singing a rock score eight times a week can trash your voice. I remember losing my voice for the first time a few weeks into my contract. Singing training for me consisted of the choir in church, the hours I'd spent messing around on a karaoke machine that I was given one Christmas, and the hundreds of hours I'd logged with Mom and Dad's record collection.

Having my voice gone in a moment was pretty terrifying. The powerlessness you feel is not easy to put into words. It makes you realize in the most profound way that any talent you may have is a *gift*. Whether it's creative, athletic, or intellectual—however it manifests, talent really is *given* to you.

We are all given a portion at the starting gate and we've done virtually nothing to earn it. "He's a natural."

HAVING MY VOICE GONE in a MOMENT WAS PRETTY TERRIFYING.

It is a gift. The truth is, some gifts come to us easily. Losing my voice is a lesson in how easily they can vanish. It is by design. There will be plenty to fight for down the line. Some things should come easy.

And you know something else?

Talent isn't everything. Talent is nice. In some instances, it is a leg up, but it's only a part of what you'll need for success ultimately. Hard work and perseverance are almost more important.

It's possible to marry a meager talent to enduring success with a strong work ethic. It is just as possible to squander a major talent with laziness and inaction.

Assess what you've got. Be honest with yourself and make the most of *whatever* you've been given.

I had a lot more developing to do and a lot more to learn about protecting my instrument if I was going to move forward in professional theater. I wasn't sure what was supposed to come next, but when I took my last bow as a member of the Broadway company of *Rent*, I was officially a young man without a dream. I did, however, make a wish that this would not be the last bow I took on a Broadway stage.

The slate was wiped clean with the realization of my wildest dream.

Now what?

THERE WERE A FEW PRESSING MATTERS THAT needed to be addressed. First, I needed to graduate from high school. A look into my transcript revealed I was a tiny bit ahead academically, and if I took advanced English and math classes at the local community college, I could graduate on time with the rest of my senior class.

I enrolled at the Community College of Philadelphia in January.

I was in school two days a week. I got a job at a grocery store to make some dough and fill the rest of the day. I got back into dance classes. I applied for colleges and prepared for the round of auditions that would accompany the application process.

I'd heard or read the name Carnegie Mellon again and again in my three-month New York adventure. It was listed in the program as the training ground for some of the people I'd come to respect most during my time there. Among them was Michael McElroy, who played Tom Collins in *Rent* while I was there.

Mike is formidable in every way that counts. He was barely thirty, with a handful of starring roles on and off Broadway, one of the most gorgeous and effortless voices I'd ever heard, and a clearly visible technical process that sustained and supported him eight shows a week. I wanted to be Michael McElroy.

Michael was also a friend to me. If he saw me doing something he didn't feel was professional, he had a way of intervening and getting me to pull back on my own reins. He wanted to get to me before anyone in management had a chance to do so.

"Pull up," he would say, and I knew what he meant.

Whenever Michael would pull me aside to pass on

knowledge or give advice, he could do it without ego or debasement. Mike didn't want to humiliate me. When he could, he wanted to help. I will always be grateful.

I tried not to bother Michael much, but every now and then I could step into his dressing room to run something by him or to ask him a question about the business that he seemed to know almost everything about.

On my last weekend of the show, I'd gone to him with my plans for what I might do next.

"I'm going to apply to colleges," I began.

"Oh yeah? Where are you thinking about?" he asked.

"NYU. Fordham. I think I'd like to be in New York."

Michael nodded slightly. He never stopped his flow. He was getting ready for the show we had in half an hour. "Go to Carnegie. It's where I went. They'll get you ready."

I had my marching orders from McElroy.

WE WERE RAISED WITH AN EYE TOWARD college always. My parents didn't care what we studied.

They didn't care what college we ultimately decided to go to. We just had to *go*. It was a minimum requirement from them.

Going back to my days in the Sad-Face Box, I'd always had a tough time with authority and the expectation of unquestioned obedience. By the time I was graduating from high school, I was so bored with the cookie-cutter, one-size-fits-all curriculum. I couldn't wait to have some autonomy in my education.

I confidently applied to theater programs at four universities. I had been training formally for about four years and informally for even longer. I had a high school résumé full of competition wins and even a Broadway credit. I thought I'd have a range of college acceptance letters and choices of where to study. I hadn't forgotten Michael McElroy's marching orders, but I couldn't deny the allure of studying in New York so that I might keep one foot in the industry while attending university.

Rejection letters came in from Fordham and NYU back to back. It threw me. I wasn't sure how to feel. My ego was bruised for sure, but over time, I've come to learn that, try as we might to knock down all barriers, every now and then we have to trust the closed door.

And so I did.

New York was out. Both feet would have to be planted in my studies.

> I'VE COME to LEARN THAT,
> TRY AS WE MIGHT to KNOCK
> DOWN ALL BARRIERS, EVERY NOW
> and THEN WE HAVE to TRUST
> the CLOSED DOOR.

I'd been accepted into the University of the Arts in downtown Philadelphia. For some, the possibility of staying close to home for college can be ideal. For me, part of the draw of attending university was getting away from home. I'm sure I wasn't the first kid to feel that way.

All my eggs were in the Carnegie basket, and when the thick, perfectly square-shaped envelope showed up at my parents' door with my name on it, I breathed a deep sigh of relief. I'd been accepted to Carnegie, and best of all, while studying in Pittsburgh, Pennsylvania,

I'd be a five-hour car ride from everything familiar and familial. Close enough to get home quickly in a pinch but far enough to spread my wings a bit.

The Carnegie chapter of my young life was about to be a defining one.

I went there thinking I knew the lessons I needed to learn. In reality, I had no clue.

PITTSBURGH, PENNSYLVANIA, MAY BE ONE of the most misunderstood of any of the major cities in the US. Known as the center of the universe of the steel industry at one time, Pittsburgh has played a starring role in the history of American innovation in technology, education, and the arts. Pittsburgh natives are tough-skinned and hardworking. The local community is made up of well-educated, super-friendly folks who pride themselves on their authenticity.

With six major universities practically next door to one another, Pittsburgh is also one of the most happening college towns in the country.

Just as the ghost of Benjamin Franklin still hovers over Philadelphia, in Pittsburgh, on any city street, you're never far from the lasting influence of Andrew Carnegie. Once the richest man in the world, he famously spent as many years giving away his money as he did earning it. Carnegie raised himself from poverty by reading and studying on his own. It made sense that his passion was to inspire future generations through the power of education and public enrichment. Evidence of that was everywhere—in the concert hall, museums, and libraries he established and the university he founded in 1900 that was soon to be named the Carnegie Institute of Technology, aka Carnegie Tech. Decades later the name was changed to Carnegie Mellon University after a merger took place between Carnegie Tech and the Mellon Institute of Industrial Research.

A major step in expanding Carnegie's dream beyond applied technology and putting Pittsburgh on the international stage came with the 1906 founding of the university's College of Fine Arts—one of the first in the United States for training in art, architecture, music, design, and drama. Famous names to emerge as a result include Andy Warhol, composer Stephen Schwartz (of *Wicked* and *Pippin* fame),

Judith Light, Cherry Jones, and Ted Danson. More recent grads include Zachary Quinto, Patina Miller, Josh Gad, Renée Elise Goldsberry, Joe Manganiello, Matt Bomer, and on and on.

When I arrived on campus in the fall of 1999, I didn't know all the bits and pieces of CMU's backstory. But a cursory glance around the campus and a walk down the hallowed marble hallways were enough for me to recognize that the School of Drama was as serious about producing leaders and innovators in the field of entertainment as Carnegie was in all other fields.

The conservatory program was more intense and comprehensive than I could have known ahead of time. Private voice teachers are selected for you when you arrive. I'm not sure how they matched teachers and students, but I consider myself extraordinarily fortunate to have been paired with Thomas Douglas in my freshman year.

With the ears, training, and instincts of a symphony conductor, Thomas taught me all about my voice. We studied for a single hour each week over the course of my time at Carnegie, and at the finish, Thomas had taught me how to preserve and protect my instrument. In the years since,

I have never lost my voice again. If Thomas's private voice lessons were the only course I took in four years, it would've been worth the price of admission.

———◆———

IF YOUR FIRST YEAR IN COLLEGE WAS anything like mine, you may have found the workload more challenging than you expected. I went to *theater* school and it wasn't all fun and games. So when the chance came to take a break from it for a minute and pursue an alternate route to New York via Broadway once more, my reaction was: *Let me think about it for five seconds.*

My plan was to be on the first thing smokin'!

It was just before the mid-semester break of my freshman year. I got a message at the main secretary's desk in the drama building to return a call from Bernard Telsey's office.

Calls from Telsey's office were always a good thing. It remains that way to this day. As New York's premier casting director, Bernie, and his office, put together the original cast of *Rent*, along with original companies of *Wicked*,

In The Heights, Hairspray, Next to Normal, and countless others, not to mention award-winning movies and television shows. Bernie was known for being unconventional in his casting choices. He is as discerning as they come and a great person to know in the business.

Not only had Bernie cast me in *Rent,* he'd made sure to get me involved in a few other projects that were in development while I was in New York. All of my earliest professional experiences came out of that office.

The last time we'd spoken was shortly before I left for Carnegie Mellon. I'd gone through a very short audition process and been offered a principal role in the Atlanta tryout for Disney's *Aida* with music written by Elton John and Tim Rice. The show was slated to come into New York immediately following the Atlanta run.

My family talked over the terms with Bernie's office for about a week. We went back and forth about salary and accommodations. We called Michael McElroy for guidance.

We weighed it all against the Carnegie Mellon acceptance letter. Ultimately, we decided that I would accept the opportunity to become a member of the class of 2003 and forgo the Disney detour for now.

Six months later, the call from Bernie's office was again about *Aida*. They were offering the same role, this time for the Broadway transfer of the show. It was a very different offer and in just six months, I'd become a slightly different kid.

I thought, *I am about to spend four years preparing to fight to walk through a door that's open right now.* And turning down the opportunity twice felt . . . risky.

I hung up with Bernie, who'd given me a few business days to think about it and talk it over with my folks.

IT WAS a VERY DIFFERENT
OFFER and in JUST SIX MONTHS,
I'D BECOME a SLIGHTLY
DIFFERENT KID.

I was pretty sure of what my decision would be. This job had my name on it. Who knew how long it would take for something like this to come around again? I could take a leave of absence, go do the show, and come back to Carnegie a year or two down the line, with another Broadway credit to boot.

It was the last weekend in October when I took the bus home to talk the whole thing over with my folks. My grandparents made the trip from South Carolina for the family meeting as well.

Whenever I came home, I would happily lug my eight to ten pounds of dirty laundry from Pittsburgh to Philly. A weekend with a free washer and dryer.

My father met me at the door, shouldered my duffel bag, and paused to look me in the eyes. He did this whenever he saw me after I'd been away for some time.

Dad told me that I would get the final say on all this. The family would weigh in over the course of the weekend. I only had to promise to listen.

I assured him I could do that.

A little while later, we took our seats around the dining table and I was given the floor to spell out the offer as it had been presented to me. My family listened first. There was a silence after I finished. My grandfather broke it.

Lennell "Lenny" Odom, *Poppy*, my grandfather, was a hilarious and indomitable spirit. In the south, during the period of his youth, the expectation on my grandfather was that after a few years of schooling, he would join the work force and contribute to the household. Poppy, who'd only completed the fourth grade, had one of the most agile and brilliant minds I'd ever known. He warned me not to place the allure of the Broadway offer over the chance to get my degree.

Though he has been gone for quite some time, I'm not sure that I've ever fully mourned his absence. Poppy passed away after a short battle with cancer about four years after this meeting. It's never made sense in my brain that such a person could ever truly be gone. Somehow, for me, there's enough of him still here that it doesn't feel like he abandoned us and disappeared into thin air. I thank God for that.

"Speedo," Poppy said in his southern drawl, using another one of the family's nicknames for me, "I want to see you walk across that stage with your cap and gown on and get that piece of paper. That'll make me jump up and down. All this stuff will be there for you when you finish."

Dad chimed in. "College is a golden opportunity, too. Remember how excited you were when you got your acceptance letter? Give yourself this time to develop. Set aside this time in your life for *you*."

I listened as I'd promised. It was an Odom united front. Mom and Grandma echoed the sentiments of the patriarchs. Even my baby sister got a moment to weigh in. I was certain to have a sympathetic ear from the youngest member of our family.

"I think you should stay in school," she said in a quiet but confident voice.

A united front indeed.

The end of the weekend came. My grandparents had already started their trek home. My dad and I sat watching a movie on television in the den, killing a little time before the hour came for me to take the Greyhound back to Pittsburgh.

Dad threw the question casually my way. "Have you made your decision? What do you think you might do?"

I considered how to break it to him. The simplest and most direct answer had to be the best way.

"WELL, I THINK I'M GOING to ACCEPT the OFFER," I SAID.

"Well, I think I'm going to accept the offer," I said.

Dad looked dumbfounded. He shifted uncomfortably on the couch next to me, put the television on mute.

I continued, "I will absolutely go back to Carnegie in a year. They will hold my slot for me."

"You won't, though," he said.

"I will," I insisted.

Dad took a cleansing breath, as if contemplating the next move in a chess match. He hadn't quite planned for this response from me. I could tell it was tearing him up, but I also believed that if it was truly my decision, then his reaction shouldn't be a deciding factor. I was prepared to stand firm. The way I saw it, the adults in my life who cared about me most were also underestimating me. They assumed that I would never return to CMU once I left. They were encouraging me to walk away from something very special with no guarantees that it would ever come around again. Maybe they'd taken my early accomplishments for granted.

"You booked this one. You will book another Broadway show, but the timing will be right," Dad stated plainly.

Easy for you to say, I thought.

He'd started this whole thing by saying the decision was mine, and I'd made my decision. I headed back to

Pittsburgh to pack up my dorm room and say good-bye to my new friends for now.

Early the next morning, far too early, I got a call from Mom on my cell phone. She'd been crying. Her voice was thin and breaking. She said she'd woken up at the crack of dawn to pray, that her spirit was unsettled and her stomach was turning. Through choked tears, Mom begged me to reconsider.

What could I do?

Half-asleep and worn down, I agreed not to take the show. But I had a condition of my own. I told my sweet mother that neither she nor my dad would ever get to play this card again. I assured her it would not work the next time, and I meant it.

That passageway into adulthood is a tricky one to navigate for parents and their children. I was somewhat resentful of my folks for a while for their highly pressurized tactics, but from where I sit today, I don't blame them. They felt something strongly and they wouldn't have been able to live with themselves if they hadn't tried everything within their power to get me to make the decision they felt was the *right* one.

As for my development, those four years were beyond price. I am talking about my development as a human being now and not just how I make my living. College and university study can be the kickoff to your adventure as a lifelong learner. If you have the opportunity to give that time of exploration to yourself, you should. All the responsibilities of adulthood will be waiting for you when you finish. Poppy was right about that. There's no need to hurry it along.

My folks also guided me to one of the most salient lessons of my whole life. To this day, I cannot be sure if taking the show would've derailed my life or catapulted me into major success a decade and a half sooner. I also can't be *certain* I would've kept my word and returned to Carnegie or if job offers would've kept coming in and school would've possibly been put off indefinitely or if I would've wound up a twenty-five-year-old burnout. What I can say is this: through this process, I learned to say no, and it'll be as valuable as your yes. Maybe even more so. It was an object lesson in empowerment that has stayed with me always.

There is a freeing power of an honest no. It's the yang to yes's yin. Balance, as always, is key.

At the urging of my folks, I walked away from a special opportunity, and though the outcome would make me a little nervous, the sky didn't cave in. Walking away angered some people on the other side of the negotiation table, with one person infamously telling me, "I'll see you in five years when you're waiting tables."

If that was to be the outcome, then so be it. Do not let your fear, or anyone else's, rob you of the power of your yes and your no. Own them both and use either as you see fit.

IT WAS an OBJECT LESSON in EMPOWERMENT that HAS STAYED with ME ALWAYS.

I had the time of my life at Carnegie. I learned and grew in ways that are *still* revealing themselves to me. I made lifelong friends. My professors taught me method and process. They taught me craft. Craft makes you reliable, and reliability gets you work.

The dissolving of any fear I had left attached to the word no has been useful to me almost every day of my life since that time.

Come what may, through the fat and lean years, you must retain ownership of your yes and your no. In many respects, it is *all* you own in this world for a very long time. Yes can come easy. No takes a bit of practice.

Your no, your willingness to walk away when something doesn't feel right for whatever reason, will be one of your greatest assets. It will set you on a path that you will own as well.

CHAPTER 4

HOLLYWOOD OR THE TOKEN

When I was a child, I spoke as a child,
I understood as a child, I thought as a child:
but when I became a man,
I put away childish things.

—1 Corinthians 13:11

 SPENT THE SUMMER AFTER graduating from Carnegie back at home in Philly for what I hoped would be the last extended stay for a while. There was a tension at home almost always by this point. Fathers-and-sons stuff.

My plan was, one more summer at home. I'd save money and then move to New York for a fresh start in the fall.

I was in my early twenties; I had my "piece of paper" from one of the top conservatories in the country. It was time to begin. It was time to pick a place on the map . . . and begin.

I always thought I would end up in New York. I went to Carnegie with Broadway in mind. I was going to be Michael McElroy.

Things had shifted along the way. Somewhere during my third year of school, I think it was, I realized I was never going to *be* Michael McElroy. I let that go in order to grab hold of something greater. Sixty percent of conservatory training happens in front of a mirror for one reason or another—all your dance classes, some of your voice classes, too, all utilize the mirror as means of teaching you how to self-correct. You learn a ton about yourself. There's no getting around it. The mirror is literal and figurative; at some point, I seized the opportunity to begin to understand the things that made *me* unique. I grabbed ahold of the opportunity to become the best version of *myself* I could be, and I never looked back.

The four years changed me in untold ways. Conservatory training was about stretching and it was also about defining space for yourself. You weren't always rewarded for it, but you were often asked to reach for things that felt beyond your grasp. Because of this boundary testing, we graduated from university with a strong sense of what we could do really well.

It's never a bad idea to take an inventory of the strengths you've developed as you push forward into the working world. You can lead with your strengths.

After four years, I knew I had the ability to steady myself under pressure. It helped in audition rooms. I was usually readily empathetic. It allowed me to inhabit characters who were different from me. And I knew how to comport myself and infuse my work with a little style. It wasn't much, but it's what I was coming with.

It's not that learning stops once you toss up your graduation cap. Quite the contrary. That chapter of conventional and structured education may be over for you, but whatever your area of focus was in school, you'll earn advanced degrees in Problem Solving, Team Building, Rebranding, Risk Assessment, Media Management, and many other subjects in life's continuous course study. The syllabus is vague, the stakes are higher, and the multiple-choice tests can feel interminable, but the good news is: you're the one handing out the evaluations at the end of a term. You will be the one tracking your development along the way. You can change course, extend deadlines, double the homework assignments, or cut them in half.

When I first set my sights on New York, I had dreams of heading back to Broadway right away even though there was a growing trend that saw the choice roles going to television and film stars. Working your way up the ranks in the theater and becoming a marquee name on the strength of your work alone seemed to be a thing of the past. Nevertheless, I had my piece of paper and a dream. I figured it was gonna be tough, but I was game.

Graduating seniors from CMU get a real entrée into the business with what's called a *showcase*. It's our version of a job fair. Most of the conservatories and drama programs will arrange them on both coasts. Students prepare a very short solo performance of some sort, and they also will perform a short scene with a classmate.

Well-established agents, managers, and casting directors attend. The hope is to make enough reliable connections out of the showcase to get a foot in the door of the industry. If not a whole foot, a toe would be nice.

After the showcase, you'll get a sheet of paper that has

a list of the people who would like you to contact them. There were kids who every casting director, agent, and manager wanted to meet. There were a few who, for a myriad of reasons, received little to no interest. And then there were the rest of us, who had . . . something. After the New York showcase results, I committed to taking the few meetings I had and making that enough.

Other professional fields have similar ways of scouting candidates coming out of college. It is a big opportunity, but I promise you it won't be your *only* opportunity. Though showcase was important, it wasn't *everything*, even if that's how it felt at the time. In the end, in a recurring theme, it was much more about what you *did* with what you were given than about what you were given.

> IT IS a BIG OPPORTUNITY, BUT I PROMISE YOU it WON'T BE YOUR *ONLY* OPPORTUNITY.

I signed with a small agency in New York and made plans to move to the city at the end of the summer. The Los Angeles showcase hadn't happened yet, and I'd already committed to New York. It's maybe a little telling of what I thought of my chances for making it in Hollywood. Before I'd ever visited, of course.

In preparation for the Hollywood showcase, we returned to Pittsburgh and retooled our performances. Many of us had spent the year getting as fit as we'd ever been in our lives. We'd spent three and a half years focused on craft, but before showcase . . . we heard that Hollywood likes 'em pretty, so we focused on pretty.

From graduating classes that preceded us, we *had* seen how Hollywood could snatch you up right from the showcase and put you on a path to superstardom. Joe Manganiello, Matt Bomer, Abby Brammell, Cote de Pablo—all had incredible showcase results and subsequent early success.

I was still very much committed to staying on the East Coast, but I thought, *Hey, if we're going to Hollywood anyway, might as well take a real swing at it, right?*

Right?!

THE LOS ANGELES LEG OF THE SHOWCASE
went well. Way better than I expected. After the performances, I had a handful of meetings to set and I was enjoying the city's vibe.

The first powerful executive I met in Los Angeles was a woman of real integrity.

Lucy Cavallo was vice president of casting at CBS. After the showcase, she invited me to meet with her in her office in Hollywood. Her walls were decorated with posters from the many hit shows she and her office had cast over the years.

Lucy spoke plainly and in a way that felt sincere. We had a loose and easy conversation about the training at Carnegie, my early Broadway experience, her responsibility and position at the network. Eventually, Lucy cut to it.

"So, when are you moving to LA? I want to put you on TV."

We've all heard the cliché Hollywood stories about charlatans and rubes. The town is littered with stories that started similar to mine but ended in a very different way. Animal instinct will be your guide for some of it at the start. Honor those early bits of information sent to your brain and your senses in a first meeting. You will sharpen your instincts and good judgment over time.

I only had good feelings and instincts about Lucy's sincerity. But if trusting someone doesn't work out the way you planned, don't be too hard on yourself. You'll only be better at spotting similar signs earlier the next time. The same is true when someone's straight with you. You can feel it as sure as anything. You'll learn to spot those signs, too.

During the showcase visit, I was on my own in Los Angeles. Three thousand miles away from home, I was taking it all in, assessing for myself. When the week was up, I would have a very big decision to make: palm trees and the Pacific or the concrete jungle. It felt like the first major decision of my young adult life. The first decision I would make entirely on my own.

As I mulled my options, I reconnected with Jacques Smith, who, like Michael, had been like a big brother to me during my time in *Rent*. Jacques had played Benny in the show. A Princeton grad and one of the most genuinely good-natured men I've ever known, Jacques was another hero. If I did decide to give Los Angeles a try, Jacques offered me the couch in his one-bedroom apartment for as long as I needed it.

The plum roles in New York are going to television stars anyway, right?

More and more I was thinking I should take the time to find out what was cracking in LA. *If all goes well, it could turn out to be the straightest shot back to Broadway*, I thought.

I came back from LA, singing a new song about seventy-degree weather, Hollywood Boulevard, and swimming pools. I felt a surprising pull west, and I saw no reason to ignore it.

Dad, however, had a long list of reasons to ignore it. When I got back to Philly and filled my parents in on the appeal of the West Coast, I was met with a dose of their skepticism and fear.

I suppose it is understandable. As a parent myself now, I can imagine how difficult it must be to trust the intuition of your child. I will always be Leslie and Yevette's child. But though they might not have been ready to admit it, I was no longer a child.

And I'd absolutely meant what I said before when we came to our understanding over *Aida*. I laid claim to making the next big decision in independence. I intended to honor that promise to myself.

Dad tried reason. "We don't know anyone in LA. What if you run into trouble? How are you going to get home?" He tried blunt truth. "I think you're making a mistake."

I respected his trepidation. He hadn't seen what I'd seen. He hadn't met the people I'd met. I barely knew a soul in the city, yet there was a calm in my spirit as I explored and tried to get the lay of the land and a feel for my new adventure. I had seen the signs for myself in Hollywood, and though they were pointing in an unexpected direction, I was prepared to put my own intuition to the test.

As a child, you very rarely get the final word on anything. But each one of us gets to a point when we have to say, *I've got this. Making decisions is my job now.*

The disagreement over the move created a rift in the relationship with my dad for many years. It was about more than the move, of course. Our stuff went way back. But the move exacerbated it.

Leaving home is a necessary rite of passage that should probably take us as far afield as we can possibly go. The first flight from the nest should entail some risk. The territory is expansive. Explore.

I moved to LA at the end of the summer with a plan to give it six months. I had twelve hundred dollars, Jacques's couch, Lucy Cavallo's office number, some training, and a whole lot of heart. Before the move, I'd touched base with Lucy's office to let her know I was making my way to the West Coast after all.

THE FIRST FLIGHT from the NEST SHOULD ENTAIL SOME RISK.

I had to account for the errors I was sure to make at some point. Making decisions on my own steam was new. I lowered the stakes of the cross-country move by reminding myself that New York was just a plane ride away. If those first six months had been awful, if I'd shown up and found the city and situations working against me, if I couldn't get solid footing, or make a friend, I told myself I wouldn't be ashamed to pack it up and try something else.

The Universe is speaking to you always if you're willing to listen. And I was listening. I was looking for any sign that I could get that this wasn't some huge mistake like my folks had feared.

On my first night in LA, I got a call to audition for a CBS series the following day. Jacques graciously agreed to drive me the forty-five minutes there and back.

The audition went well, they asked me to return the following day, and Jacques agreed to drive me once more. I read for the producers that next afternoon, and two hours later they called to offer me the job.

My intuition was confirmed. And I had my "sign" in about forty-eight hours.

The role was only a recurring one-day guest star as the fingerprint technician on *CSI: Miami*, but to me it represented much more. It was the beginning of adulthood. My intuition hadn't steered me wrong. The by-product of trusting Lucy was the confirmation that I could trust myself.

THE HOLLYWOOD GAME IS NOT SO different from any other competitive field. Supply and demand often rule the day. You can choose to play the game and fit the demand, or you can dig deep and offer something your field has never seen before and stand out. The latter is much harder, and for a newcomer, much riskier.

When I arrived in Hollywood, there was arguably more opportunity for black actors and for actors of color than ever before. There is even *more* all these years later. But there was still a tendency toward tokenism. The lure of tokenism in my business, and in any business, really, is that it's easy. Hiring a few, or the single, minority player can keep you "safe" from a certain type of scrutiny or criticism. The one Asian on a team, or the single gay person, or the one physically disabled person, or the lone black character, can make a project appear woke or edgy because of its *diversity*. But I would submit that if you have a person from an underrepresented group on your team and you aren't tapping them for their unique and varied perspectives and contributions, it may be tokenism. And if it's tokenism, it's always a missed opportunity.

Tokens are window dressing mostly. They're props. You can make a living as a token, but you'll long for more.

I showed up in Hollywood and tacitly agreed to play this game. More than that, while I longed for more, for some time I allowed myself to think this was all I would ever be used for.

I'll be the token, I thought. *I'll work twice as hard to give these stock characters and caricatures a reason to exist that goes beyond filling quotas and serving functions, but it is what it is.*

I am certain that I spoke the words at some point, but to *think* them was enough to make it my reality on and off for almost a decade. It was limiting and it was painful. I cast a reductive vision for myself at the outset, and it was ten years of maturation and growth before I could dismantle and demolish the pattern for myself.

In the beginning, you audition for almost every call that comes in. If it doesn't cross some moral or ethical line for you (remembering you must retain ownership of your yes and your no), your answer is almost always yes to a potential opportunity. There were times when I was vying against other brothers in the Hollywood shuffle to play a three-dimensional human being, but there were more times when we were in competition for the token. This process is definitely BYOD. The *D* stands for dignity.

There were times when I could bend to expectations and there were times when I couldn't quite twist myself into enough of a pretzel to make it palatable for myself or my potential employers.

I remember testing for a pilot early on. In a scene where I was out to dinner with the two women who were my bosses on the show, I was getting the note back from producers and casting that the scene wasn't working. "Can he be more street in that scene? We just need him to be more street."

Just how *street* were they expecting me to be at a meeting with my bosses in a five-star restaurant? The answer was: very.

I couldn't make it happen. It was a step too far for me in that moment.

IT WAS a STEP TOO FAR for ME IN that MOMENT.

What I have to own, what I have to take responsibility for, is the vision at the outset that over time began to do damage. As a young man, my thoughts were born out of strategy, ambition, and survival instinct—and in my initial vision, I sold myself short.

Don't sell yourself short. You will meet people along the way who will be lining up to place limits on you. You don't need to beat them to the punch.

Vulture did a popular recap of each episode of a short-lived network series I was on. Onscreen I was doing my best turn in a thoughtful, honest, and three-dimensional performance. It was sometimes at odds with the material I was being given, but I was doing the best I could.

Still, I wasn't prepared for the moment I read the recap following the episode in which my character was initially introduced for the season-long arc I had on the show. The author cuts to the chase and gives me a "funny" nickname that'll be used in all the recaps moving forward: *"reserving an especially loud shriek for the actor playing Token . . ."*

In reference to a moment of screen time I shared with a black actress and dancer: *"'I don't think they're doing much sleeping,' says Token's sister Tokenetta . . ."*

In front of the camera, I try to lead with my humanity. Sometimes I fall short, but it's usually where I'm coming from. My best efforts in front of the camera didn't matter. There was no mention of them ever. I was there to serve a function and the function came before my humanity. I abhorred the function.

Token has no past and Token's future is dubious, so Token's present is threadbare.

In my tacit cosign to gain access and make a living, it hadn't occurred to me that "Token" wouldn't be limited to just a function onscreen. The reality was painful enough, but when I saw the world *renaming* me . . .

It was time to put away childish things.

CHAPTER 5

PERMISSION TO FAIL

I don't ever lose. I either win or I learn.

— NELSON MANDELA

*I've never seen any life transformation that didn't
begin with the person in question finally getting sick
of their own bullshit.*

— ELIZABETH GILBERT

THERE IS SPACE FOR *SAFE* AND *bland* in every industry. I had two feet firmly planted in that space.

Guided by instinct and faith at the start, moving to Los Angeles was the riskiest thing I'd ever done. But in a short time, I'd gone from daring to boring. I was so busy playing the game that I forgot why any of it mattered in the first place. That was as good a reason to make a change as any I've ever heard.

During those first five years or so in LA, I had gotten the hang of things. I was booking a fair number of jobs.

My parents could regularly turn on their television in Philadelphia and see their son, which was a thrill for them. For me, too, I admit. But there was still a lot missing.

Everything changed in an instant the first time I really gave myself the room and the permission to fail spectacularly.

EVERYTHING CHANGED in an INSTANT the FIRST TIME I REALLY GAVE MYSELF the ROOM and the PERMISSION to FAIL SPECTACULARLY.

Like anything worthwhile, failing spectacularly takes a bit of practice, and I had none. I look back at my college years, and this is my one regret. I made plenty of mistakes in school, but I wish the environment had encouraged and provided more room for failure. My training hadn't included any focus on audacity. Nothing in my training encouraged or spoke to the value of taking real risks and so I wasn't in the practice of taking any.

The tuition came as a particular hardship for my folks, and I racked up student loans in the shortfall of financial aid. I took the sacrifice seriously. I wanted my transcripts to reflect the seriousness with which I approached my education.

I did really well and graduated with honors from Carnegie Mellon University. I learned what was expected of me, and, in most cases, I delivered. Because of the grading system in place and quite possibly (I say in truth and with respect) the egos of some of my professors, there's no premium placed on risk. That meant wasted valuable time, because risk is *much* harder once you leave campus and stakes go up. More room should be made on our college campuses for trial and error.

You should be encouraged to fall on your face, to fail in service of an ideal or a strong impulse.

When you find yourself on the ground after a big leap, you dust yourself off and commit to failing smarter next time. The path to moments of greatness in your life will be paved, in part, with your spectacular failures. Keep going.

THE PATH to MOMENTS of GREATNESS in YOUR LIFE WILL BE PAVED, in PART, with YOUR SPECTACULAR FAILURES.

Get shame and fear out of your periphery as soon as you possibly can and keep going.

It is never too late to learn to risk.

———◆———

ACCESSING YOUR EMOTIONS CAN PUT YOU in touch with a fuel that can push you into high performance. For better or worse, anger has always been tremendous octane for me. It's a tricky one, though—high doses can have adverse or even the opposite desired effect and siphon off energy a little at a time instead. Learning the right equation to optimize forward momentum and also learning how and when I need to take some deep meditative breaths and get on the hunt for an alternative fuel for a particular moment has been part of my life's journey. But it was anger that pushed me to the point of my first major breakthrough.

I was in my midtwenties when I got the chance to work with a hero of mine, Mr. Billy Porter. Billy is a maker of things beautiful in the highest order. In his storied and impressive professional career as an entertainer, he's been a director, a singer, a curator, an actor, a dancer, a writer. Though if you were to ask me, or any of Billy's students, his work as a teacher and mentor would rival his achievements in any one of these areas. Billy is known as a Tony and Grammy award–winning star around the world, and I've learned a great many lessons at his feet. Chief among them was the time he pissed me off so bad I was forced to fly.

We were in Philadelphia with a new theater piece Billy had written and was directing. The central character was one he'd initially conceived for himself but after some consideration he called to offer it to me in his stead. I am still humbled by the thought. Billy created an opportunity and an avenue for *me* at a time when not many were doing it for *him*. A decade later, Lin-Manuel would do a similar thing for an entire cast of underused and barely used talents in *Hamilton*. I think it's just about the holiest thing you can do in this business—leading another artist to the well of good gifts within them. I hope there's a special place in heaven for people who make this a part of their life's work.

Being Alive, Billy's show, was an evening of songs, curated and rearranged from the works of Stephen Sondheim, using

a small cast made up entirely of African-American performers. We had premiered in Westport, Connecticut, just a
couple of months earlier. Philadelphia was the next stop in
trying to iron out flaws in the ninety-minute evening.

Being Alive had potential, but ultimately we never got
it quite right. Along the way, though, a disagreement
about the treatment of a particular moment in the show
presented my first real runway for failure. I did not meet
the opportunity with gusto.

There was a moment deep into act two where Billy
had written what I deemed a classic Billy Porter moment.
The writing and arrangement of the tune pointed to *big*
singing at the ending. There were vocal ad-libs over an
ensemble of singers. The moment called for passion, fer-
vor, fire. On an emotional scale, ranging from one to ten
(ten being lifting the roof off the theater), Billy was looking
for a ten.

The probem was—I was never comfortable at ten. It
was dangerous and unpredictable out on that limb. I pre-
ferred making calculated, intellectual choices throughout
an evening and arriving at a predetermined emotional
ending in the cleanest and safest way possible. Using my

intellect along the way would ensure that no one could accuse me of not knowing what I was doing up there; it allowed me to maintain my sense of control.

Billy, keying in on my resistance, starts to ask me to relinquish my tight grip of control over the moment. My thought is. . . *Nah. This is a sure thing. What you're asking me to do is not. What you're asking me to do is* risky.

I've worked to increase the size and power of my voice for years. It's gotten better, but it is what it is. Had Billy stayed in the role, I had no doubt that he would've played the moment perfectly. Billy would've torn the roof off and the house down. That's what *Billy* did. That's not what *I* did.

In a notes session after an early performance, Billy says, "Leslie, I see you making the choice to downplay that moment in act two. I'd love to see you try something else tomorrow night."

Nah, I think.

The next night: "Hey, Leslie, I would still really love to see you take the stage and your space in that moment. It's staged and written to support you. Just give it a try tomorrow night."

"Okay, I'll see if I can make it happen," I say. Though I have no intention of making it happen.

From my fearful perspective, what I was doing worked and there was never any way I was going to deliver the moment Billy was asking me for, in the way that he wanted. I didn't have what that would take. And if I could avoid facing the inevitable failure, I was more than happy to.

Billy comes to my dressing room after the next performance to talk through a few things. Eventually, we get to that moment again.

"I love everything you're doing, but I see and feel you resisting my direction here. What is that about?" he asks in earnest.

"I'm not you, Billy," I blurt out. "I'll never be you. I know what you're asking me to do, and I cannot deliver on that moment the way you would."

Billy looked like his heart broke for a moment. His eyes softened and he grabbed me by my shoulders. "I would never ask you to do it like me. I don't want you to be me," he said in the kindest tone he could muster. "I want you to find your sixth gear. I know it's in there and I feel you resisting. I don't know why and I am not sure how to help you. You have got to trust me. You have to let me see it, whatever it is, and if it doesn't work, we will try something else."

I heard him in the deepest and truest part of myself. I knew he was right. It was only fear that was stopping me from taking the leap at this point. He was building me up the way great coaches do but my insecurity was too close to the surface to admit it in that moment. I couldn't let it go right then.

Later that night, I downloaded with a castmate about the session Billy and I'd had. I was angry at Billy for making this a sticking point. I was angry that he couldn't let it go. I was angry that he'd made it about trust (because that is exactly what it was about). Billy had called me on the carpet and there was no way around it this time.

In my anger, I surrendered. I told my castmate, "I'm going to do it tomorrow. I'm going to go so far in the direction that he wants that it's never a conversation again." I didn't know why my teacher wanted me to look like a fool in front of a theater full of strangers, but I committed to it anyway. I committed to failing.

What Billy was asking of me could quite possibly tank my performance and the ending of the show along with it, but if that was what he was willing to risk, so be it. I was full of fuel and ready to fail spectacularly, if only to show my mentor how wrong he was.

I WAS FULL of FUEL and READY to FAIL SPECTACULARLY, IF ONLY to SHOW MY MENTOR HOW WRONG HE WAS.

The next evening, as the moment approached, I was furious. I was sick of the conversation. I was ready to show Billy once and for all that I knew my own limitations and that it was he who lacked trust in me. I sailed past ten on the emotional scale and went for the eleven. I screamed. I flailed. I jumped. I ran. I cried. I let go. I flew. I soared. It shook me.

I had never felt so free in my work in my whole life. I knew nothing of this type of abandonment. It was a little frightening. And it was exhilarating.

My teacher was right, right, right, right, and I am so grateful he didn't give up on me. To this day, I tell him often and without reservation. The ceiling I'd built for myself was broken that night, and the only reason I ever look back is to say thank God. In my willingness to fail, I flew instead.

YEARS LATER, LA PRESENTED AN OPPORTUNITY to fail spectacularly as well. But this time anger wasn't the fuel. Curiosity was.

I'd grown so tired of the rut and niche I'd carved out for myself. I was tired of the uninspired work I was producing. I wasn't challenging myself and I was so bored.

Then I got a call to come in and read for the lead role in a new Wayans brothers movie. The Wayans have a history of making satire and parody as good as anyone in the business.

My first thought was—*I'm funny sometimes, but I don't know if I'm Wayans brothers funny.*

I took the audition anyway.

I spent the next day working on the material, trying to come up with "bits." A funny walk, maybe? A funny talk? It was all pretty lame. I put the material down for a bit to clear my head. Unexpected inspiration and clarity hit me like lightning. I picked up the material again to be sure that what I was inspired to do would work.

The comedy made sense to me for the first time. I fought genuine laughter as I continued to try to learn my dialogue. I wrote notes to myself all over the script; cues that would keep me on track and remind me to honor my instincts and follow-through—even when old habits and fear crept in and tempted me to a safer place.

DON'T BE FUNNY. YOU ARE NOT FUNNY. DO NOT MAKE THEM LAUGH. THIS IS A DRAMA. PLAY IT LIKE BRANDO WOULD PLAY IT.

Simple enough. This was my bright idea. As I saw it, the characters were in a world that they took literally and completely seriously. My guy had no idea he was in a Wayans brothers satire. My guy was living his life with a documentary camera crew following him. Simple enough and scary enough.

I drew a line in the sand for myself. This would be my first professional risk. Failure wasn't going to be a by-product of the goal. Failure *was* the goal. If I went in and they didn't laugh once, if they called my agent after I left the room and said, "He was seriously the worst actor we've seen today. Not only is he not getting this job, do not send that actor in here again"—it was only a win if it went as far as that. That's how *not* funny I had to be. I was prepared to defend my work and be dropped by my representation if it came to that.

Young actors are taught to feel utterly disposable. You're always fearful that you'll be abandoned if you displease.

But this was *it*. If I was to make myself proud and pull myself out of the inertia and boredom that had begun to sap my energy, this was the stand I had to make. If any of the worst-case scenario outcomes came to pass, I'd have my freedom in their place. What's a risk if there aren't any consequences?

The audition room didn't laugh when I started. They didn't laugh as the scene progressed. They asked me to read one of the scenes again. I was *more* serious the second time through. The sillier the moment, the more I sank into the drama. The more I sank into the drama, the more they leaned in. I caught a smile from Marlon out of the corner of my eye, a small laugh from Shawn.

The tension in the room dissipated. They worked with me for fifteen minutes or so. They were kind and generous, it was way more fun than I had anticipated, and then it was over.

In the parking lot, I got a call that I would be testing for my first film on the Paramount lot in a week. *They* thought I'd *potentially* been Wayans brothers funny. The Universe is speaking to us all the time.

IT WAS THE BIGGEST PROFESSIONAL RISK I'D TAKEN up until that moment, and none of the worst-case scenarios came to pass. In fact, it was just the opposite, and more important than any of that was the fact that I'd taken enough ownership over my own path to give *myself* the permission to fail spectacularly.

In the end, I lost the role to the other actor who tested named Damon Wayans, Jr., a nephew in the family lineage. All good. Damon is damn funny and has never rested on laurels. He works hard and has made a ton happen for himself over the years. I am a fan.

But when it was all said and done, mine was the only evaluation that mattered. I administered the test. I'd be the only one who would know if I passed or if I failed with flying colors.

I hope you'll give yourself permission to do the same as soon as possible.

Deeper creative freedom waits for you on the other side of your fear.

CHAPTER 6

THE
TURNAROUND

Not everything that is faced can be changed,
but nothing can be changed until it is faced.

— JAMES BALDWIN

'VE NEVER PLACED A LOT OF credence in astrology, but when I was first told about the phenomenon known as the Saturn Return, I had trouble shaking the warning I was given. A friend who had been through a challenging time at about twenty-nine years old said that the orbiting of Saturn around the sun and its return to where it was at the time of his birth had brought on major changes and thrown everything about his life into question. It was a time of change and big choices, he said, about what we really want to make of our lives for the *next* thirty years.

He got my attention. The truth is that change was already in the wind, and I knew the time had come to either dream a bigger dream or get busy creating a new reality.

Not all the changes that had taken place had to do with conscious decisions on my part. One of them—meeting Nicolette Kloe Robinson when I was twenty-seven years old—happened by a grander design than my own.

My mentor Billy Porter was coming to LA to direct a short run of *Once on This Island*, a magical love story, for a small but reputable theater company in town.

"What are you doing?" Billy screamed at me over the phone. I knew the tone and tenor of the man well by then.

"What *should* I be doing?"

Billy was always looking to share opportunities, so whenever he had a project on the burner, he'd look for ways to include me. If something was on my calendar, I'd make it disappear.

"I'm coming to town to direct *Island*. I need you to assist me."

"When do we start?"

There were two weeks of preproduction. I got Billy coffee, I took notes for him, I made demos of the new musical arrangements he'd created. Being around Billy was always worthwhile, always a good hang. He taught and led by example, and I could count on him to push me creatively 100 percent of the time.

When auditions began, my role shifted to that of a reader. That meant I became the scene partner for every actor who auditioned. You can learn a lot sitting on the other side of the table all day in an audition room.

On our second day of seeing people, a young woman reading for the role of Ti Moune, the central character in the musical, caught everyone's attention. Lithe and lit up from the inside, a then-nineteen-year-old Nicolette Kloe Robinson walked into the room and anyone with a pulse took notice.

She was in her junior year at UCLA in their theater department, and I thought she was a major discovery. Nicolette's pure heart rests right on her sleeve. You only have to know her for a few seconds before you find yourself caring about what happens to her. That quality felt like an essential characteristic for our central character if you asked me, but I wasn't in charge.

Nic didn't get the role, but I distinctly recall thinking,

The business is so small, I am sure to run into that girl again.

THE BUSINESS *is* SO SMALL, I AM SURE *to* RUN *into* THAT GIRL AGAIN.

A few weeks later, we were almost done with rehearsals and were just about to move from the rehearsal room into the theater when a cast member's husband's health took a turn for the worse. She had to drop out and tend to her family immediately. There were something like three days left before the production had to be ready to be in front of paying customers. Billy had to think fast.

He shifted some things internally and brought the talented UCLA student in to play a different role from the one she had auditioned for. Since I was Billy's assistant on the project, it fell to me to make sure Nicolette was up to speed and comfortable.

Easiest job I've ever had. Nicolette was so gifted and learned at lightning speed. Her disposition was breezy— Los Angeles sunny—and the space around her was calm and focused. There was nothing not to love.

Nic and I would meet during backstage traffic patterns and slow dance before our next cue. I'd wait in the wings for her to finish her big moment in act two just to bear witness to her growth from show to show and marvel at her sparkle in the light. A peck on the cheek had become a kiss on the lips by the closing weekend of *Island*.

A week after parting at the theater, we made plans to hang out and . . . we haven't stopped since. She is the best friend I've ever had and the kindest and most generous person I've ever known.

A pro tip on love, if you'll allow me: when choosing a partner, choose someone better than you. You'll feel lucky to be building alongside someone you respect, and it'll keep you striving to be the best version of yourself always.

You may not have met that person yet, but they're out there. Love is a risk like any other. Have faith. Let go of the past narrative of near misses, and err on the side of *you never know*.

MY LONGEST AND MOST MEANINGFUL

relationship: another gift for which I have Billy Porter to thank. His hand wasn't directly responsible for bringing us together, but he set the stage. These are people you keep close.

Over the years I've made it a habit to grab and hold on to mentors. Ever since Mrs. Turner, I've always found them easy to identify.

Preferably, you want them in close proximity. Face time with your mentor will be important in your development. You need someone who is willing enough to share with you. The best mentors will open and read from the private pages of their lives so that you may learn from their mistakes. Sure, you can glean valuable info from their success, but their failures (if they're generous enough to share them) can save you years of heartache and help you make informed decisions when you find yourself at a crossroads—in my experience.

When you meet someone you respect and admire, do your best to hang on to them. Be in touch. Listen well and apply the lessons they help you discover when you see fit.

Be prepared for gaps along the way. There are times you may find yourself without a mentor or someone close who has perhaps trod a similar path. These are the times when you'll stand in the gap for yourself. You'll show up for yourself and collect the memories from your triumphs and spectacular failures to share with the young person who will look to *you* as a mentor soon enough.

You may find that a mentor who's achieved goals similar to your own doesn't quite exist in the way you've imagined. All that means is . . . lace up! *You're* the person. You will blaze the trail and become the mentor you've always dreamed of.

I SAT IN THE FRONT OF MY MENTOR IN 2011, shortly before my thirtieth birthday, and the future felt gravely uncertain. I was depressed and in real need of advice from somebody who could help me see my way out of a painful spot. After weeks of weighing my options, I had all but made up my mind to end my acting career in favor of something—anything—more stable. I looked to Stuart K Robinson to guide me toward the stability I craved.

When I pulled into the driveway of his house a few years prior to this moment, I knew there was a great deal I could learn from Stuart, but I hadn't predicted that he would become someone whose counsel I would seek regularly in years to come. At the time, I had been on a few dates with his daughter, Nicolette, and the dinner that night had been carefully planned for me to meet the whole family and (hopefully) pass muster.

Meeting all the Robinsons brought out a sense of home and family for me that has only deepened since then. And meeting Stuart opened my eyes to new possibilities for my own path. Stuart managed to put two kids through college, and buy a home, and a vacation home, and take his wife out to dinner every now and then, and he did it all somehow without ever becoming a household name.

Obviously, I was familiar with the African-American actors and entertainers in Hollywood who achieved superstar status against the odds. Who wasn't? Will Smith, Samuel L. Jackson, Whoopi Goldberg. Some you know by first names alone. Denzel. Oprah. These superstars have names you've heard often and bodies of work you know extremely well.

You wouldn't really hear about the blue-collar success of someone like Stuart outside of his large but mainly local sphere of influence.

But Stuart had *made it* in my eyes. He started out as an actor and then made the move to other areas of the business. He found success in casting, teaching, public speaking, and even as the COO of a major commercial agency in Los Angeles. He built a life for himself and his family in this industry and found a way to successfully sustain it for forty years.

Yeah, I knew Stu could teach me a lot.

We'd come to share quite a bit over the years, but his finest hour as a mentor and friend came at that very moment in 2011 when I needed it most.

Some of us have a sense that we have to figure out everything on our own. We mistakenly think that being in need of help or advice is a sign of weakness.

Give your friends and mentors the gift of showing up for you.

Can you identify the three to five people who love you most? They want to help you. They want you to win. Reach out. The first step out of any depression or stagnation is asking for help. One vulnerable conversation with Stuart and I was never the same.

The uncertainty and feelings of being stuck were different from what I'd felt before. After the major breakthrough and other lessons of growth in my twenties, I was no longer plagued by the lack of inspiration in my work. I'd seen a change in myself in front of the camera. I was taking more risks, and the risks saw my booking rate increase. I was booking relatively big jobs and making fans at the networks. If the phone was ringing, usually it meant I was working. That was good enough for me. What I couldn't figure out, what I couldn't stand anymore, was all the time when the phone *wasn't* ringing.

The final straw had come in connection to a pilot I'd recently done. It's true I had done pilots before but there was something different about this one. I had fought for the role and won it after seven or eight auditions. The show was interesting and sexy with a winning cast and producing team attached. I had my hopes set on a series pickup and a six-season run. Short of that I was sure that being part of such a high-profile project would get the phone ringing even if we *weren't* picked up. I was wrong. After it was all over and the pilot didn't become a series, I found nothing had changed. The needle hadn't moved at all. I was in exactly the same spot. The lack of control was enough for me to want to throw in the towel and focus on something—anything—more secure.

WHAT I COULDN'T FIGURE OUT, WHAT I COULDN'T STAND ANYMORE, WAS ALL the TIME WHEN the PHONE *WASN'T* RINGING.

The fact that I was a part of the small percentage of union card holders in Los Angeles to find themselves employed in the entertainment business meant that I was achieving success. But when even success starts to feel like failure, it's time to make some changes.

Stuart had found tremendous success in other areas of the business. The face time I'd requested was not to get Stuart to tell me how I could *make it as an actor.* I was done with that. I wanted the opposite of the life I'd been living.

Stu, having heard me out, nodded in silence. He then took a long sip of his water, taking extra care with his word choice. I'm sure he could see and feel that I was pretty fragile and wound up. The truth is that I was in "a bit of a state."

Stu confirmed and reassured. He said of course I had the freedom to quit and try something new with my life. He said that we could talk about other possibilities if that's what I wanted to do. And then he spoke the words that would change everything: "But I'd love to see you *try* before you quit."

His words felt like a punch in the gut. A well-intentioned punch, but a gut punch just the same.

He wanted to see me try? What did he think I did in these audition rooms? How did he think I'd managed to gain any ground in the nine years I'd been in LA? Still . . . I listened.

"You don't think I try?" I asked in earnest.

Stu drove the point home. "I think you do extraordinarily well when you're called upon. I think you show up and you're confident because of your preparation." He paused and asked the million-dollar question, "But what did you do on your own behalf today? Did you do anything other than wait? Did you call anyone? Did you send an e-mail? You have great relationships with people who know your worth. Do they even know you're out of work?"

Whoa.

The questions embarrassed me because I knew exactly what he was driving at. I wasn't doing nearly enough to help myself. It was a total blind spot. I'd been sitting on my hands. I could feel the clouds parting as my mentor went on.

"You could get a band together and go to all the local coffee shops. They'd love to have live music. You haven't been singing at all." He reminded me that I had never explored commercials or voice-over work. "I've invited you to take my class for the last year. You could start there."

I was a bit ashamed not to have thought of any of this sooner. I almost couldn't wait for our session to be over so that I could get to work *for real*.

Stuart taught a commercial class in town that was renowned. It was probably only because he was Nicolette's old man that I had ignored it for so long. I enrolled in the beginner's class and started the following week.

My class was primarily made up of novices and newcomers. You could tell sometimes by the wardrobe or the drawl. Mostly you could tell from the sunny dispositions. These people were excited. They were stoked to be getting their commercial careers under way, and to be learning the secrets to success from the man they'd heard so much about.

I was less sunny, of course. *Pros aren't sunny.*

My heart and ego were still pretty banged up and bruised—but I thought I was hiding it well.

The first lesson came early.

Stuart told us we were auditioning for a toothpaste commercial. He sent us to the front of the room in groups of four and went down the line with a camera as he asked innocuous, casual questions while filming each response. *What's your name? How tall are you? What's the last great movie you saw?* Or—*What's your favorite dessert?*

Sometimes there was a follow-up question and sometimes there wasn't. The whole thing took maybe forty-five seconds a person. He made his way through everyone in the class in twenty minutes or so.

I'd been clever and charming, I thought. Simple enough. I didn't know what the test was exactly, but I thought I did all right. As far as I could see, there was varying success from the class on our first assignment. Some of the newest and most inexperienced members of the class couldn't think of an answer to Stu's question at all. They'd smile bashfully and search for words. Some would answer confidently and go for a joke to ease tension.

I watched each one and tried to see it through Stu's eyes. I had no idea what he'd be looking for, but I tried to guess. *Pros are easy to spot*, I thought.

"All right, so—" Stu began, when everyone in the class had been recorded. "There are times in a casting office when we're extremely busy and doing other things while the audition tapes play silently in the background. We're looking for a spark, a transmittance or warmth and feeling, even in silence." He muted the sound. We watched playback of the toothpaste exercise we'd just done, in silence.

What message are you sending out even before you open your mouth? What soundless story is your body telling when you enter a room?

It was astonishing to see how fresh and inviting the newcomers were. A bashful and honest smile was worth a thousand canned safe responses any day. With the sound off especially, the novices were killing it.

Then it gets to my forty-five seconds on the tape and . . . I could see so clearly the difference between the newcomers and me, and it wasn't the fact that I was "a pro."

The difference that I could see was as plain as day. There was a film of corrosion and jadedness over me that had to be stripped immediately. I'd misjudged the newcomers. It was me who had much to learn.

YOU WOULD CALL the SUNNY NEWCOMER BACK TEN out of TEN TIMES BEFORE YOU'D WANT to SEE the JADED GUY AGAIN.

Years of heartbreak and rejection had made me guarded. I was tight and tense, and it wasn't being hidden well at all. You would call the sunny newcomer back ten out of ten times before you'd want to see the jaded guy again.

When I broke it down for myself later that night, I came up with a plan of action. I made a commitment to myself to come *rushing forward* in the rooms I was invited into.

No hanging back. No waiting to find out if it was "safe" before bringing what I have to the table. *I am bringing it regardless!* Moving forward, I would risk the rejection and take more responsibility for the energy I was carrying with me into rooms. I would be as fresh and as free as the newcomer.

The lesson of the Saturn Return was a reminder that we each have a choice. Do we let the past dictate our future? Or do we come *rushing forward* with the best we have to offer?

A WEEK AFTER MY VERY FIRST CLASS WITH Stuart, I booked two national commercials and a great part on the Don Cheadle vehicle for Showtime called *House of Lies*. After the second and third classes, it was a part on *Supernatural*. A week after that I had to leave the class completely because I was on a plane to New York as an added cast member on a new series for NBC, *Smash*.

For the rest of my life, I will credit Stuart K Robinson for getting me off my couch. I made a commitment to myself that I would never again sit in inaction, waiting for the phone to ring. I was ignoring at least half of my responsibility as a businessman.

What are you ignoring today? What did you do to help yourself today? Who did you call? What did you read? Did you take one step toward something that makes you come alive today?

If you're willing to take one humble and meaningful step toward making a dream come true, the Universe will take two.

You will be aided. You will get the help you desire and desperately need. Take the step. You'll win or you'll learn.

CHAPTER 7

HAMILTON
ACT 1:
OUR
TOWN

*An artist spends their whole life trying to get back
to the place where their heart was first opened up.*

—SOME GENIUS

**WENTY SECONDS. EIGHT BARS.**
That's how long it took in July of 2013
to feel the irrepressible tug of history in
the making. The lights had barely gone
down on the first-ever staged reading of *The Hamilton
Mixtape* at a festival of new works on the Vassar College
campus in Poughkeepsie, New York.

The reading started, and in a blink I was transported
right back to that record store in Philadelphia where I first
heard the entire *Rent* cast album standing on my feet at
a listening station—that place where my heart had first

been opened up. I knew right then that I'd been waiting for my whole artistic life to feel the feeling once more.

Nicolette was on the campus for the summer, working on a piece she loved. I visited often to watch my favorite performer in action. I'd catch other new shows in performance whenever I could. On the festival's schedule there were two performances listed for *The Hamilton Mixtape* at the one-hundred-seat Powerhouse Theater. Both sold out almost immediately.

This new work was from the creative team behind *In the Heights*, after all. As its composer and lead performer, Lin-Manuel Miranda had won Tony and Grammy awards for his work in the semiautobiographical musical celebration of the Manhattan neighborhood where he had come of age.

In the Heights had closed a couple of years earlier. The industry eagerly awaited the sophomore outing from the talented young man and his cabinet of collaborators. The pre-excitement meant that even in the development stage, scoring a ticket to see the new work was nearly impossible. Not even a tweet to Lin could get me in.

I had made friends with a few ushers during my frequent

trips to see Nic. My powerful friends with flashlights saw to it that when the lights went down at the start of the reading, I was able to grab an empty seat in the very last row of the tiny theater.

The *Mixtape* included only act one at the time. Act two was still very much a work in progress. But the first twenty *seconds* gave us a glimpse into something extraordinary. It was multilayered brilliance made all the more powerful and resonant because of the well-chosen multiethnic cast of performers giving their hearts to the material. Lin's score was so bold and fresh and confident. For me, hearing it for the first time is what falling in love feels like.

I had met Lin only briefly before. Our paths had crossed a handful of times at social events or at the theater. I knew that *The Hamilton Mixtape* was not a fully realized show yet, but what they had already was so special. What they showed us that afternoon at Vassar was once-in-a-lifetime special.

By the end of *The Hamilton Mixtape*, I was emotional for all kinds of reasons, some of which I can barely explain.

I know now that part of my reaction surrounded lingering questions I had about *translation* and the things that get lost along the way when going from one language to another. Less than a year prior to taking my seat in the back of the small theater at Vassar, a hundred-year-old text had illuminated a cultural blind spot for me. I'd been wrestling with existential questions it presented for months . . . and though I wouldn't have been able to explain how or why in that moment, *The Hamilton Mixtape* felt like the answer.

FOR ACTORS OF COLOR, A LARGE DE-termining factor of our success in the business is closely related to how good we are at translation.

Flashback to the hundred-year-old text—I was cast in a benefit reading of Thornton Wilder's lasting and iconic *Our Town* for the Actors Fund in New York. The one-night-only event would feature the talents of B. D. Wong, S. Epatha Merkerson, Celia Keenan-Bolger, and others whom I had long respected and admired. These types of nights can be a lot of fun, but preparation is key. They're well attended by industry insiders. The evenings are relatively low stakes but very high pressure. You want to feel good about how you did because there are no do-overs.

A couple of days before the first rehearsal, while preparing to play George, the young male lead of the piece, I found myself smack-dab in the middle of a mild identity crisis when asking myself the question: *But who am I really?*

You see, Thornton Wilder's beautifully wrought *Our Town* was never intended to be *My* Town. By that I mean, even though *Our Town* tells the story of the fictional Grover's Corners, New Hampshire—a stand-in for a kind of Everytown, USA—when looking at context clues from almost every major production of the seminal work, there don't appear to be any people of color drawn in Wilder's quintessential American town.

Fine.

Our Town, which follows the lives of George Gibbs and Emily Webb and those of their families, and some of the town's other residents, did have universal dimensions, to be sure. The play is set in 1901 and takes place over a period of twelve years. Narrated by an omniscient "Stage Manager," the script takes us through different life stages that run the gamut from the mundane to the peaks of romance and marriage, and the lows of death and loss. At the time of its debut, *Our Town*—staged with no scenery and no curtain—was considered to be a radical departure from traditional theater.

After a thorough read of the play, it was time to begin the process of finding honest, empathetic pathways to a credible portrayal of George. It always begins with as strong a vision as I can conjure of myself inhabiting the world of the play. But this time, try as I might, I couldn't get a clear vision.

I couldn't apply much of my American experience to Thornton Wilder's New England town. In my deep dive, I had serious doubts about whether Mr. Wilder wrote his play with an eye toward the *color-conscious casting* of his seminal work at some distant point in the future.

Wilder wrote the truth as he imagined it. He wrote the truth about a small town of white strivers at the turn of the century. It is through his detail and specificity that he is able to tap into powerful and universal truths about the human experience. Obviously, plays about the specific and unique concerns of a town full of black people at that same point in American history would have an entirely different language and tone.

For context, 1901 saw the first publication of Booker T. Washington's *Up from Slavery*, about his life's journey from child slave to nationally renowned orator, philosopher, educator, and author. Just five years earlier in 1896, *Plessy v. Ferguson* cemented legal segregation of the races, with a landmark decision handed down from the highest court in the land. It was a line drawn in the sand and on our buses, train cars, restrooms, diners. It set the stage for the future American horror stories of the Jim Crow South. In 1905, W.E.B. Du Bois founded the Niagara Movement, a civil rights organization that preceded the NAACP, whose prescient ethos called for an end to racial segregation and disenfranchisement. All around the United States, there were riots rooted in the protest against racism and its ugliness.

The mundane existed for black people in 1901, too. We cooked breakfast, lunch, and dinner as well. We went shopping and dancing. Black children played hopscotch and football in the street, too. But the more I read and tried to imagine, the more it felt like my casting and Mr.

Wilder's text were at odds. It was the trickiest translation job I'd ever been given and I wasn't sure it was going to work at all.

Am I a Black George in Thornton Wilder's Our Town? *Am I to investigate the way these scenes would play differently as Black George? Won't my race impact the power dynamics in the play or dramatically alter the temperature in some of these scenes? Or . . . am I meant to ignore all this?*

Am I a white person for the evening? Am I, instead of Black George, "Black George in Whiteface"?

My imagination had posed the question: *Who am I really?* Integrity demanded that I hunt down the answer.

Logical solutions eluded me. I had no clue how I was going to translate Mr. Wilder's text into anything that came close to a truthful rendering onstage.

In the midst of something of a downward spiral, I paused, and after some deep breaths, the voice of my wiser self took over.

This is an experiment and no one has the answers. You have been invited into the room to search for the answers alongside your collaborators.

You're afraid. Guess what? So is everybody else.

This experiment will work or it won't work, but you've been invited into the room to explore. The exploration is the mission. You have the permission to fail.

YOU HAVE the PERMISSION to FAIL.

I had to remind myself of it then. I have to remind myself of it today. We all have patterns we repeat. Learn to recognize your patterns early. Maturation is only learning to spot these patterns and having the self-discipline to make different decisions once you do. Practice will make the process faster.

Life has shown me again and again that the answers to some of the most profound questions can only be revealed during the expedition. Those first risky, wobbly steps will require some heart and your humility.

We found our way to *Our Town*. The audience received us well, and I'd had a transformative experience along the way. I carry the lessons with me today. Representatives from Thornton Wilder's estate came to see the one-night-only benefit. One commented that it was one of the most poignant and moving versions she'd ever seen.

Nicolette and I had just gotten married. This was the first piece I'd worked on since then, and I was able to connect emotional dots of love and loss in ways that I never knew were possible for me. There was a new emotional depth I'd found in my life that I was able to bring to my work.

As for the translation of the text, we discovered that there were more than enough cognates in the Universal language of the heart and the language of our shared humanity to bring a collective light of truth to *Our Town*. The new emotional depths and possibilities came as somewhat of a revelation to me, and I couldn't wait for the opportunity to test the limits once more.

"OCTBURR" WAS THE SUBJECT LINE OF AN e-mail that came from Lin in the fall of 2013.

    Leslie!

    I hope this email finds you happy, healthy,
    and creative.

So I'm writing Act Two of *Hamilton* as fast
as I can (it's never fast enough for my
tastes, but I digress) and we're hoping to
sing through what I have so far on October
8. I'd love to have you join us. We'd
rehearse Saturday the 5th (take Sunday
off), Monday the 7th, and the morning of
Tuesday the 8th, and sing through it that
afternoon.

This is nothing so formal as the Vassar
performance you saw. No audience, just us
and Jeffrey Seller to see where we are. Are
you around/available to play? Lemme know.

Siempre, Lin-Manuel

I didn't want five minutes to lapse without a response from me. I checked my calendar and hit reply: *I'd love to*. By the subject line, I got that I'd be reading the role of Aaron Burr.

The schedule and material were in my in-box a few hours after that, and I got to work immediately.

I figured I had an ace up my sleeve. There were just over two hundred people who'd seen the first act of *The Hamilton Mixtape* at Vassar. Coming into the week, I had an advantage in that I knew firsthand how incredibly special Lin's piece was, and I knew how challenging it would be. Professionally,

I've never been more game for anything in my life.

PREPARATION IS the SIGN of YOUR INTENTION.

Preparation is the sign of your intention. You can allow your preparedness to speak *for* you in rooms you care about.

By "Octoburr," Lin had probably put in hundreds of hours of preparation and hard work. As I saw it, my impossible task was to try to catch up. There was no better way for me to show my affinity for the piece than to learn the words and rhythms exactly as the man had written them and, beyond that, try to begin to understand the reasons and impulses behind *why* he'd written them.

This was a time to go for broke and a time to find the courage to lay it all on the line.

At Vassar, I thought that *Hamilton* was the smartest, freshest, most brilliant piece of original material I'd ever seen. And now it was in my hands. My personal goal for my very first week of work on *The Hamilton Mixtape* was simple: to make them never want to see anyone else in the role of Burr ever again.

WE DID SEVERAL READINGS OVER THE NEXT year, each one more clearly in focus and more complete than the last. I watched the cast get assembled one by one. For me, there was never an actual audition to be in *Hamilton* after the e-mail from Lin. Instead it was more like a protracted two-year audition before the Broadway opening, which was only the beginning in many respects, but the surest end to the development process. For two years or so I was focused on staying available and doing everything I could to knock it out of the park every time one of those presentations was scheduled.

There were no assurances that you would make it to the next *reading*, let alone to the Public Theater or to Broadway. What you did know was how lucky you were to be invited into the process at such a delicate time and how lucky you were that you might leave a lasting impression on the thing. We looked to our director, Tommy Kail; to our musical director and arranger, Alex Lacamoire; and to our choreographer, Andy Blankenbuehler, as lighthouses.

Hamilton seemed to have a healing and disarming emotional power from the outset. During more than a year and a half of readings and rehearsals, I witnessed the reactions of hardened, jaded professionals from various facets of the entertainment business as they reconnected with childlike wonder and sometimes tears—as I had the first time I saw it.

Love was my way into Lin's work and to Aaron Burr.

LOVE was MY WAY into LIN'S WORK and to AARON BURR.

I didn't feel the need to approach Burr as a villain. That wasn't how Lin approached him in the writing. Anyone who writes a character a song like "Dear Theodosia" or "Wait for It" is not looking at that character as a villain. Burr and Hamilton were close from the start. They had come up together, they respected each other, and, different as they were in temperament, they had a lot in common. At nineteen years old, neither would have believed they'd end up on those dueling grounds more than twenty-five years later.

I wanted to be so led by love throughout the proceedings that I would be surprised by those final moments in the show. I wanted to be *shocked* by the ending every time. My goal, every time we arrived at the denouement, was to hope against hope that things could turn out differently. Kind of like the end of *Romeo and Juliet*, when you imagine there might be a last-minute twist to save the kids from themselves. You think, *Not this time, not tonight*.

My goal with Burr was to lead with his humanity. I would forgo being *liked* by our audiences and settle instead for being *understood*. I wanted to make him as ugly and beautiful and flawed and interesting as the people in the seats who'd come to witness.

In the process of developing the show, I was certain that something about the role and the experience was changing me from the inside. The work was making me a better friend, a better husband, a better man. I felt closer to God and closer to that bottomless creative well within all of us than I'd ever felt before. With Burr, I recognized that Lin was giving me the opportunity to become the type of actor I always admired.

Nothing could keep me from seeing this thing through to the finish. Nothing. Except a few months before we opened at the Public Theater, that was exactly what a new series on NBC threatened to do.

***STATE OF AFFAIRS* LANDED IN MY LAP AS** one of the easiest jobs I'd ever gotten. I went in to read for the casting director on a Tuesday. She filmed the audition in her office. By the following Monday, I had the job.

A pilot had never happened for me like that before, and it hasn't since. The whole process had been so painless, I could hardly believe they were serious when they called to offer me the job. You usually jump through hoop after hoop for these types of things. It takes weeks or months. You're usually trying to convince them that you're up to the task. This was almost too good to be true.

I'd auditioned because, well, why not? The show would shoot in New York. My bank account had been giving me the side-eye for months. My agents knew not to send me in for anything that would conflict with *Hamilton* (I wouldn't even consider something that would put my participation in jeopardy), but my commitment to *Hamilton* in its development phase had financial ramifications. Doing some television "uptown" while I fed my artistic needs "downtown" made a lot of sense. Television is really nice work if you can get it. It isn't easy, but I wouldn't be the first actor in town who kept a role on television during the daytime and worked at night in the New York theater. For many, it's the only way the equation makes sense. Off-Broadway theater is a tricky financial proposition, no matter how brilliant the material. Television work can ease the hardship.

If the pilot was picked up, as a series regular I would supplement the $800-a-week paycheck in *Hamilton* at the Public Theater (which gets cut nearly in half after taxes, commissions, and expenses) with my *State of Affairs* payment of $35,000 an episode (which also looks a lot different after deductions). That was a model that made sense to me.

The only problem was that *State of Affairs* never intended to keep production in New York if it got picked up. The show would move to LA, and, as a contracted series regular, I would have to move to LA with it. I didn't know that piece of information until the announcement of the pickup happened.

The role of a lifetime in the most masterful piece of original work written for the theater that I'd ever encountered was about to slip from my grasp on a technicality.

For me, *State of Affairs* was a great job. *Hamilton: An American Musical* might've been one of the great loves of my life. Artistically, it was what I had been waiting for since my heart was first opened and I'd started down the path years ago.

State of Affairs was a contract that would guarantee $500,000. At the time, the *Hamilton* agreement guaranteed less than $15,000. Financially, it wasn't even a contest. But Nicolette and I prayed, and I kept my focus on moving toward the thing that was making me feel most alive.

Once I'd made the decision that *Hamilton* was what I wanted to do, advice poured in from respected advisers. Some suggested that I hire a lawyer to negotiate my way out of the *State of Affairs* contract, others recommended a PR maneuver or bringing more agents into the conversation. But the reality was that I had no legal recourse if NBC decided to enforce the terms of our agreement. After months of consideration, as elementary and ridiculous as it may sound, I realized that asking nicely was the only option I really had. I also had to admit to myself that if someone at NBC said no, for whatever reason, *Hamilton* would probably be over for me.

Any misstep in my conversations with NBC could have serious career ramifications and risk burning bridges at one of the major TV networks. Not having the conversation would risk letting the role of a lifetime slip through my fingers without a fight.

There is no risk that isn't tied to a consequence. You assess and make sure you can live with the ones you can foresee.

In an e-mail to Bob Greenblatt, the chairman of NBC Entertainment and someone who's turned out to be a real friend, I poured my heart out with as much honesty as seemed appropriate in the delicate situation:

```
No one knows the power and relevance of a
vital American Theater more than you, Bob.
I suspect that no one knows its pitfalls
and challenges better than you do. You
know what a rarity it is to come across
```

a genuine masterpiece. If one is lucky—I
mean truly truly divinely blessed—at ONE
point in your career you are invited into
the room at the development phase of an
Angels in America, or a *Sunday in the Park
with George*, or *Rent* . . . think about the
very first performers who were given the
unsullied, never-before-seen-or-heard-of
perfect librettos of *Gypsy*, or *Fiddler*,
or *Dreamgirls* . . . they are a part of
history. Their contribution to the craft
and to our industry was not only inspiring
and entertaining but extraordinarily
necessary.

Hamilton is that timeless and necessary
work. This show is going to revolutionize
our industry once again.

I am desperate to be a part of it.

I realize that this email bucks protocol.
These are matters that are usually left
to agents and managers but I really wanted
you to hear from me. It is out of respect
for our friendship and the incredible
amount of kindness you've shown me over
the years that I wanted to try to explain
what all the fuss is about and why this
project means so much to me.

Bob and the producers of the show let me out of my contract with no penalties. They wished me luck and they meant it. When *Hamilton* tickets were most scarce a year and a half later, I found a way to repay them.

IN THE END, I THINK WHAT MADE THE connection to Lin's work so deep for me was the *language* in which it is written. For one of the first times in my life as a professional actor, I felt like I was standing center stage in a work that was written in my *tongue* even though the men and women that we were portraying were, in most instances, as disparate from us as could be imagined.

The story was theirs at its inception. But this time around, the rhythms, the syncopations, the dance and the vibe, the pulse, the movement, the moment—this time around—was ours.

This town was ours. No translation necessary.

CHAPTER 8

HAMILTON ACT 2: THE NEW AMERICAN DREAM

But, just for a moment now we're all together . . .
just for a moment we're happy. Let's look at one another . . .
It goes so fast . . . Oh, earth, you're too wonderful for anybody
to realize you.

— E M I L Y
in Thornton Wilder's *Our Town*

HEN WE GOT WORD THAT THE
Broadway transfer of *Hamilton* wouldn't be
happening until the following season, after
our record-breaking run off-Broadway,
I have to admit it was a tough pill to swallow. Lin and the
producers made the decision to give the show more time
to cook off-Broadway; rushing ran the risk, they felt, of key
production elements not coming together quickly enough
and endangering the quality of the show. That being said,
Hamilton had amassed one of the strongest word-of-mouth
campaigns the city had ever seen, and I wasn't alone in

hoping a move uptown could come sooner rather than later. At that juncture for me in early 2015, more time only meant more time struggling to make ends meet.

We were in the middle of a bitter, lingering winter in NYC with winds, inclement weather, the works. I invested in a pair of long johns and a new sweatshirt. These would have to do, as there was no room in the budget that season for a new winter coat or boots for me or for Nicolette. Traveling by taxi was also a luxury we had to do without. The commute from our apartment in Hell's Kitchen to the Public in the East Village could be brutal.

Most of the cast was in a similar position. There were articles being written and lots of talk on the outside saying we were fools not to capitalize on the heat and buzz of the moment by transferring to Broadway as quickly as possible. Seemingly overnight, *Hamilton* had become the hottest ticket in New York City. The scarcity of tickets, due to the three-hundred-seat capacity of our off-Broadway home, fanned the flames of the frenzy. There were those who said that if we thought that same attention would be waiting for us whenever we decided to move uptown the following season, we were deluded.

We paid our dues that winter. The off-Broadway run wasn't easy for any of us, but it sure did serve to bring us closer together.

> ## THE OFF-BROADWAY RUN WASN'T EASY for ANY of US, but it SURE DID SERVE to BRING US CLOSER TOGETHER.

Over the development process, I'd had the unique pleasure of watching a cast of supernovas assemble one by one. The small ensemble at the Vassar reading was made up of almost entirely different players than our cast at the Public Theater. Lin, Daveed Diggs (Lafayette/Jefferson), and Chris Jackson (Washington) were the only cast members who'd remained from *The Hamilton Mixtape* reading that I saw in the small theater in Poughkeepsie. I was added next in the "Octoburrfest." The developmental reading after that saw the arrival of Phillipa Soo in an expertly sung, brilliantly restrained, and miraculous performance as Eliza Hamilton. The workshop after that brought us Oak (Okieriete Onaodowan in the roles of Hercules Mulligan/

James Madison), Anthony Ramos (John Laurens/Philip Hamilton), and Renée Elise Goldsberry in her star turn as Angelica Schuyler. They were each so distinct and skillful. It was clear when a new member was added to the crew permanently. The keepers were always easy to spot. It wasn't just talent that would get your foot in the door and keep it there. Your humanity played a part. It was generosity and kindness; it was intelligence and fearlessness. Lin and Tommy were recruiting a championship team.

Jasmine Cephas Jones (Peggy Schuyler/Maria Reynolds) was added before we started rehearsals at the Public. Another winner. Stunning, with a confidence that belied her youth.

Together, along with an ensemble of fourteen other triple threats, we did close to one hundred and fifty performances of *Hamilton* off-Broadway.

What they were unable to give us in money at the Public Theater, they gave us in artistic resources, warmth, and kindness. It was a glorious space for creating new work, and they supported us as a company and as individuals in every way they could think of.

Oskar Eustis, who runs the Public Theater, leads with

unmatched passion and ferocity. I've never met an enemy of his. Eustis is one of the beloved.

I'm not sure if anyone, outside of the creative team, has seen *Hamilton* more times than Oskar and his brilliant wife, Laurie. Through development and our off-Broadway run, they were in the audience many, many times, and I always found their presence comforting and focusing.

Oskar would find me backstage afterward at some point with tears still in his soulful eyes. The refrain was always the same. "You know it's never like this, Leslie. You have to know that. It's never like this."

"I know it, Oskar."

"This is special, comrade."

"I know, Oskar."

And I really did.

When we finally closed the show at the Public, five months after we opened, it was a joyful time. Spring had returned to New York City. There was expectation in the air. We had six weeks off and a Broadway theater waiting for us.

DON'T EVER STOP GETTING BETTER. MAKE it your mantra. Make it habitual.

Coming into rehearsals for the Broadway run, I think we all felt the strong desire to level up. There was no reason to deny that we'd made something special downtown and that it had found an audience. It was connecting with people viscerally and gaining influential new fans in almost every theater-loving group. But no one in that room had any desire to stop growing and learning in the interim between productions.

DON'T EVER STOP GETTING BETTER. MAKE it YOUR MANTRA. MAKE it HABITUAL.

The scheduled Broadway opening night fell on my birthday, August 6, which, after the road I'd been on to make it to that very night, somehow felt like a cosmic wink. A sign that everything was going to be all right. Maybe more than all right.

There were absolutely no guarantees at any point during the development process. There was no promise of a Broadway run when I answered Lin's "Octoburr" invitation. There was no guarantee that I'd be kept in the role even after I'd walked away from the television series for the production at the Public Theater. We had indications that the show was impactful and that it could find its audience if given the opportunity, but the worldwide embrace of the material after the Broadway bow was not something any of us could've predicted. We kept our heads down and in the work.

For my part, before rehearsals began for Broadway, I took on the dreaded but necessary task of watching and critiquing my work. There was a digital copy of the off-Broadway show that was floating around. It was a tool used solely for the purposes of bringing understudies up to the task of stepping in for performers at a moment's notice in the case of illness or emergency. It was also a great visual reference to improve on Andy Blankenbuehler's intricate spacing and stage pictures.

You have to be both a harsh critic and strong advocate for yourself.

There are tremendous advantages to being able to get some perspective on your own work. It's tough. But you have to find the objectivity to look at your work and become the teacher, the coach, the mentor for yourself when the moment arises.

I didn't make it past ten minutes of the tape. I shut the thing off the moment it became clear to me what my work needed to be in the two-week rehearsal process before our Broadway opening. In the off-Broadway run, I'd been so focused on the emotional journey and the more technical demands of Lin's score that I hadn't made strong enough physical choices for Burr. I had barely landed on any. I didn't have much time to add the crucial element, but I couldn't move forward without drilling down on this piece of the performance I'd all but ignored.

YOU HAVE to BE BOTH a HARSH CRITIC and STRONG ADVOCATE for YOURSELF.

I approached Jon Rua, one of the extraordinary movement specialists in our ensemble, and asked if he could find time during the few off hours we had to help me make stronger choices and take the performance to the next level. Jon and I worked with a camera in our sessions. He helped me create the beginnings of a movement vocabulary for Burr. We talked about how to better use, fill, and inhabit the space. I'll always be grateful that Jon was willing to take the time.

The result was a more fully realized and three-dimensional performance uptown. When I was at my best, it was a full-bodied investment in the evening's proceedings, pinky toes to hair follicles.

The work isn't over until it's over. You either fine-tune and keep making it better until they rip the pencil from your hand, or, once you intuit that you've finished and that you've conveyed what you intended to convey in your work, you put your own pencil down, step back . . . and triple-check.

THE WORK ISN'T OVER UNTIL IT'S OVER.

We kept the things that worked and jettisoned the things that didn't. The off-Broadway to Broadway transfer was all about the edit. We had the time to make it better. We had the time to release the grip on something that really worked and grab ahold of something that could really, *really* work.

This was the group of people crazy enough to try.

EVERYTHING ABOUT THE EXTERNAL WORLD changed for us after *Hamilton* opened on Broadway. History was cool. Broadway was mainstream. People cared about who we were and what we had to say. It was all new. Where it gets tricky is how you allow those external changes to affect you on the inside. Success can change who you are so easily. Especially if you don't already know who you are. I am grateful that I'd lived some life, and spent a little time in the wilderness before Burr found me.

Tommy Kail, our director, went to great lengths to preserve the sanctity of the work space. Early on, he gathered us together.

"I can't control what happens outside of here. I know how noisy it is for you all."

We were only just getting started, and the distractions were many and extreme.

"Inside this theater," Tommy went on, "let this be our sanctuary. In here, we just get to do our show."

Tommy helped us preserve and protect the magic of *Hamilton*, making sure the theater remained a holy space—assuring that in the eye of that hurricane we could always find quiet.

FOR ME, *HAMILTON* WAS MY FIRST REAL BRUSH with the AMERICAN DREAM.

For me, *Hamilton* was my first real brush with the American Dream. I'd gone to Hollywood a decade earlier in search of it. All these years later, I could see that every triumph and every failure, every lesson learned along the way, was available for me to access and use to ensure that I made the most out of this moment. A Broadway musical about the Founding Fathers—a piece of art in part about slave owners and their American Revolution—bought me freedom. The American Dream had a new spirit and a new context for me now. Lin-Manuel, Daveed Diggs, Chris Jackson, and all my brothers and sisters at the Rodgers had given the dream a new face.

Hamilton tapped into what theater can do on its highest level. Lin-Manuel understands how to musicalize the highs and lows of the human experience. *Hamilton* is human rites of passage set to music. In the span of the musical, we essentially cover childhood, abandonment, adolescence, loneliness, bravery and valor, war, falling in love, getting married, having children, jealousy and envy, betrayal, death, loss, and redemption. When you get to the end of the show, there is so much life the audience has gotten to live together. Together with the storytellers onstage, there is so much ground you've covered, you can't help but feel connected. It opens you up for catharsis, for that spontaneous rush of emotion.

And isn't that what our love affair with the theater is about? It is about catharsis. We go into a darkened theater to sit next to strangers and feel something. On Broadway, actors have their days off so that at night they can come to the theater and do onstage what we are afraid to do, what we are not emotionally equipped to do, or what we aren't allowed to do in our everyday lives.

Actors are our avatars. They are our stand-ins. When a performer stands onstage and bares her soul, she bares her soul for all of us. When a man stands on a stage and lets his heart break, he lets it break for all of us. There is an invitation to participate, but we are also free to observe and learn. We elect them to do us this service—our theater stars and our movie stars. The same is true of the great singers. We elect them. I'm thinking of Marvin Gaye, and Smokey Robinson, and Barbra Streisand, and Tina Turner, Bruce Springsteen, Jay-Z, Kanye, and Nina Simone. They don't just sing for us, they sing *for* us. Bruce is the voice of a generation. Jay-Z is the voice of a generation. Marvin is the voice of a generation. They are the chosen representatives of a group of people.

If you're ever curious to know who an artist is, get to know their fan base—get to know the people they sing for.

Art has to occupy a space of significance in civilized society. We translate the vitality of the human experience through the art our society produces. We translate the pain and discord, the joy and sadness, and majesty—all of it—through our art.

I think *Hamilton* did this. It is, at once, one of the easiest and hardest things you can set out to do. Lin set out to do it with his pen. He recruited a room full of people willing to carry that vision from the page to the stage. We gave *Hamilton* back to New York City on August 6, 2015. They gave us their open hearts and the whole world in return.

IN THE SPRING OF 2016, AFTER OVER FOUR hundred performances of *Hamilton* the musical in New York City, the Tony Award nominations were announced. The awards season in general can be a heady time. We'd been through it in part once before with the off-Broadway run.

There are "Best Performance of the Season" lists that you're included on and some you are not. Once the awards season begins, you can't help but have it in your periphery, but you'd do well not to make it your main focus.

I was hopeful for the Tony nomination for sure. But in all honesty, I had come so far with *Hamilton* that I didn't want the nomination or lack thereof to blight this blessing for me in any way. I knew nothing was owed to me in that moment. I remained hopeful but not expectant and tried not to lose sight of the fact that the whole thing was fleeting.

The morning of the nominations announcement, Nicolette and I cut our phones off and went to our favorite New York diner for breakfast. We ordered pancakes and waffles and locked in a memory of how good life was in that moment, sitting at a diner, with zero Tony nominations between us, and the best pancakes and waffles in New York. If life was to remain this way for a little while longer, or forever, we were going to be okay.

On the walk home from breakfast, we turned our phones on and . . . full voice-mail in-boxes and text message after text message let us know there was cause for celebration. Not just for me, but for so many of my castmates. *Hamilton* had received a record-breaking number of Tony nominations, with individual nods for me, Lin, Phillipa, Daveed, Renée, Chris, and Jonathan Groff, our King George III.

The awards were to be given out on June 11, 2016, at the Beacon Theatre. The weeks leading up were about savoring and letting go. They were about celebrating what all the preparation and sacrifice had brought to us. And they were about letting go of any expectations for the night of the eleventh. They were about savoring the fact that we got to have this victory lap as a little family, which is what the cast had become by then. And they were about preparing to say good-bye to *Hamilton* and Burr and make space in my life for whatever adventure would be next.

I couldn't hold on to Burr forever. My yearlong commitment would end at the top of July and I knew there would be many, many more talented, underused, and creatively starved men after me who would come for their own revolution on the stage at the Rodgers.

I COULDN'T HOLD ON TO BURR FOREVER.

I remember when I arrived at the Nederlander Theatre to begin my *Rent* adventure. Most of the original cast members were long gone, but their powerful intention, their love—the spell that they'd cast—was everywhere you looked. They were still there. Jonathan was still there. Those of us who came behind them ate and drank at the table they set.

As I prepared to exit stage right in a few weeks for the last time, it felt like we'd cast the spell as a company. It felt like we'd done our part to make this an equitable, welcoming, and wonderful place to work for what would hopefully be years and years to come.

At the time, the night of the Tony Awards was rivaled in excitement only by our wedding day. Nicolette and I arrived at the Beacon Theatre, dizzy and electrified. We were so happy to be there.

Lots of people will tell you that they've been practicing their acceptance speech since they were a kid. In the mirror, with the hairbrush. I get it. People asked me if I was that kid, and truthfully, I wasn't. I have never practiced my acceptance speech.

What I *have* practiced since I was a kid and my mother made me write notes of gratitude whenever someone did something kind for me—when Mrs. Turner asked me to write what was most important to me and assured me that people would care, when they gave my grandfather a year to live—is the love and care you put into saying thank you whenever you are given the chance.

Time is not promised. Say thank you in exactly the way you intend to when the moment arrives.

That was the thing I was most grateful for that night—there were so many people who'd encouraged and inspired and carried me all the miles to the podium on the night of the Tony Awards. When my name was called, my only job was to mention as many of them as I could and to say thank you from the bottom of my heart. Simple.

Gratitude has a drawing power all its own. And nothing can keep you from making it a daily practice.

⸻

I LEFT THE RICHARD RODGERS THEATRE weeks later with a tired body, a full heart, friends for life, the prefix "Tony and Grammy Award winner" to my name, the richness of these memories, and a tremendous sense of pride.

As a body of strangers, over the course of some time together, we'd touched greatness. And in our finest hour as practitioners, we'd been present, we'd been vulnerable, we'd been kind, we'd made something that mattered.

The willingness to fail led us here. The willingness to risk led us here. Love and trust led us here. I was a witness. I'll carry the experience and the gratitude with me always.

CHAPTER 9

PERMISSION TO PROSPER

Don't count the days. Make the days count.

—MUHAMMAD ALI

T'S NINE P.M. ON A THURSDAY night in October 2017, and I've just made my way into the boxing gym where I train as many days in the week as my schedule allows. For whatever reason, the gym's unusually quiet for this time of night.

As I wrap my hands and tug on my gloves to get ready to hit the big bag, I have to laugh at how few people who know me well could have predicted that I'd take so wholeheartedly to boxing. Sure, I'm somewhat competitive when it comes to working out but I've never been intensely involved with any particular sport.

So, why boxing?

For starters, keeping off the pounds is a *lot* harder with the absence of the three-hour cardio bomb I used to get eight times a week. I've had to intensify my workouts just to maintain.

Experienced fighters will tell you about the mind/body/soul integration of a great session in the gym. I am discovering all of this for the first time.

Boxing is this stripped-down, primal experience that can be almost meditative. Gabe, my coach, is part Jedi, part yogi. My favorite repeated refrain from Gabe comes whenever I'm in bad form or when some fundamental he's repeatedly shown me isn't clicking once again. Gabe reminds me, "Les, relax your shoulders." Nine times out of ten, it is all I need to hear to get me back on track.

I go through my days now hearing the simple reminder from my middleweight urban sensei. I am often surprised at how the simple self-correction can help root me in the present. Tension evaporates from my jaw and my chest. I am free to do my best. I am out of my own way. The relaxation brings old and new lessons into focus.

FOCUS HAS SHARPENED WITH SOME TIME and distance between me and the comet.

There should probably be a twelve-step program.

Hamilton the Broadway musical was a hard habit to kick.

It took me about a year to sober up completely after the trip.

I walked around in a stupor for awhile. Here, but not here.

In time, I felt ready to commit to starting something new.

In time, I felt I could do so without feeling the need to compare and measure new projects against the phenomenon.

In time, I was able to be on my new ish. And it felt right.

BUT EVENTUALLY, IT was TIME to HITCH MY WAGON to MY OWN STAR.

The *Hamilton* logo is fitting. Hitching my wagon to that glorious star paid off beyond anything I could've dreamed. But eventually, it was time to hitch my wagon to my own star. As circumstance and situations from the past had shown me the importance of giving myself the permission to fail, this time around it would be about giving myself the permission to succeed.

In the days and months after the show, I put most of my energy toward creative independence.

I knew that music was the thing I could do if and when the phone ever *stopped* ringing. I used whatever goodwill I'd garnered from my time onstage—whatever "chip" the success of the show had given me—to get a band of brilliant musicians together and get to work.

A week after my final performance, the fellas and I began a three-week residency at a club downtown. There are six of us, including me. Five pieces and a vocalist. In a week, I'd gone from thirteen hundred screaming and devoted fans at the Rodgers as part of the *Hamilton* ensemble to one hundred and twenty-five very, very polite people in a tiny room in downtown NYC, as a "solo artist."

Even so, I loved the intimacy of connecting with a much smaller audience. I loved the creative control and the freedom of expression.

With new dreams of the Kennedy Center, and Carnegie Hall, Madison Square Garden, and the Hollywood Bowl, we filled the calendar with dates around the country. We practiced. We recorded two LPs and saw them both reach number one on the Billboard jazz charts. Failures along the way have been a teacher and pushed us forward and we toast the hard-won incremental successes whenever they grace us. We were, and *are*, most certainly on our way.

Burr's credo was to wait—for the moment, the opened door, the invitation. In *Hamilton*, Burr spends *years* waiting for a chair to be offered at the table in the "room where it happens."

Patience and timing will play a part in your ultimate success for sure. But I found the happiness and the consistency I wanted for so long at the exact moment I decided to build my own table and my own chairs.

No one has to give you permission to be entrepreneurial in creating opportunities for yourself. You don't have to wait to cast yourself in the starring role in *your* narrative and then take action on your own behalf. With vision and leadership, you'll attract a team of empowered supporters and advisors. Their success will be inspired by yours.

Giving yourself permission to prosper will also challenge you to know your worth—especially when negotiating on your own behalf and asking for what is fair. This doesn't mean you have to become overly money driven or attach numerical values to your dreams. What it does mean is that as you prepare to enter or elevate yourself in your chosen field, the more financially literate you become, the better you'll be able to pave the way for your own prosperity.

Permission to prosper also asks you to define what success looks like to you. It looks different to each of us. The more clearly defined, the easier it will be to recognize when it shows up.

I'VE SEEN AN EXPANSION IN MY DREAM LIFE. *Who* I dream of and who I dream *for* expanded the day Nicolette and I welcomed our Lucille in the early spring of 2017.

Lucille Ruby was born in Santa Monica, California, in the small hours of April 23.

Nicolette labored quickly, with tremendous courage and

a determination hadn't before seen in my small-framed, sweet wife. Even the nurses were impressed! Nicolette was extraordinary, as was the tiny light we welcomed to the world that Sunday morning.

We named her Lucille after her maternal great-grandmother—a woman who wisely fled Vienna, Austria, to America in advance of the most unspeakable horrors of WWII.

Early in our relationship, while working in Europe, Nicolette and I made a trip to visit "Litzi's" childhood home. Lucille Baum was a woman with an irrepressible spirit, kind eyes, and a will as strong as steel.

I DREAM for LUCILLE JUST as MY FATHER DREAMED for ME.

Ruby is also a family name. It belonged to my mother's great-aunt. In old family pictures she's a woman with great style and a killer smile. But Nic and I figured there could be no harm in connecting our little light to iconoclastic Rubys like Bridges and Dee—even if solely in name.

Your name speaks before *you* do.

In a way, it's your first compass upon arrival. It says something to you and to the world about the dream your parents cast on your behalf, and the wish they made for you at the start.

I dream for Lucille just as my father dreamed for me.

I was around twelve years old when my father gave me the nickname *Sammy* in tribute of another *Junior*, Sammy Davis.

A nickname was Dad's subtle way of telling me he believed in me.

Dad's present to me on the night of my Broadway debut in *Rent* was a teddy bear wearing a customized sash that read, "Good luck, Sammy! Break a leg."

Through the course of writing this book, I've gained new insight into Dad's strengths as a parent and gotten more clarity about where he might've fallen short.

Mom taught me to love by loving me unconditionally. And early on, long before I was aware of it, Dad had cast a vision for me, his namesake, that was limitless. He handed down the affectionate nickname of a legend and a triple threat who, in the course of his life and unparalleled career in entertainment, removed all labels and gave himself permission to write his own story and his own ticket.

The nickname was Dad sending a message to me that he thought, maybe I could do the same. He didn't harp on it. He let me fill in the blanks.

There is something powerful about what a parent dreams for their child. It doesn't always end up as the parent intends, but the dream itself—the vision you hold for your kid until they can hold it for themselves—is so important.

I know that Lucille's experience in the world is not mine. Where she'll go and what she'll see will probably have little resemblance to where I've been and what I've seen. Even so, I am actively dreaming a dream for her, holding a vision and a space for the kind of a woman I hope she grows up to be. Her mother dreams alongside me. We grow the dream with each passing day. We dream in size and in Technicolor of the influence Lucille and the young women of her generation will wield in this world. They will leave their mark. The world will make room for them. And when they don't, our girls will unite and continue to make room for themselves.

I am in no rush, but the day will surely come when we will hand over the dreams and visions we've fostered for our sweet Lucille. Eventually we will hand them over to the young woman herself. This too will be part of her inheritance.

She will edit, reshape, and reimagine the dream as her Taurus heart demands. Our job is only to make them wild enough and large enough that she may spend her hours and her years in joyful pursuit.

Who are you dreaming for today?

WHO ARE YOU DREAMING for TODAY?

WHEN YOU ALLOW YOURSELF TO VISUALIZE your own possibilities, it is amazing how clearly and how fully they can be manifested.

A decisive change on the *inside of you* will eventually undoubtedly change the world *around you*.

I wish I could've shown the guy on the couch six or seven years ago what his life was going to look like the second he got off that couch and into action. Every single day, I can strive for more clarity and specificity of my vision. And every single day I can take a single step toward seeing that vision manifest.

There has been a steady wind at my back since being off the couch. When I prayed for guidance or asked for it from friends, I have been aided and encouraged. Whenever I've taken my one step, the Universe has always helped me take two.

I believe the same will be true for you.

I am rooting for you and your rise!

Give yourself the permission to prosper today.

Relax your shoulders. Begin.

SERIOUSLY

I will not allow one prejudiced person or one million or one hundred million to blight my life. . . . My inner life is mine, and I shall defend and maintain its integrity against all the powers of hell.

—JAMES WELDON JOHNSON

**N THE YEARS SINCE THE NIGHT** I stood onstage at the Richard Rodgers and wondered how—in the time that's passed since the walk home, on which I conceived of our conversation—what has continued to elude me has been *balance*.

I get a handle on it, and two months later I am facing something or someone that I've been neglecting, and I have to do my best to get a handle on it once more. I've been intentional in those times and successfully pulled through.

But relationships fray with the jostling.

They are delicate things.

Families fracture.

Home is the one place I do not want to face the effects of failure.

So we search for the solutions. We fold in the ones we like best. And we press on.

ALMOST HOME NOW.

I am desperate to finish my tiny book. I promised to write it. I said I would get it done in the time they allotted. It's not a big book but the commitment and investment has been total.

I want to put the final punctuation mark and my pencil down as fast as I can but I feel as if there is *one* more thing I need to say. It has yet to be said in these pages and it is the necessary counterweight to inspirational speak about achievement and possibility. In the service of balance:

A commitment to "failing up" does not trump systemic and institutional racism.

When looking at the tasks we have before us as citizens we must handle our most troubling societal ills with the seriousness they deserve. The more serious the *sickness*, the less likely you are to find the cure over the counter.

A commitment to risk or to "failure in the spectacular" is not an override key for sexism or homophobia or transphobia.

Only our commitment to citizenship can do that. And compassion. A collective commitment to compassion could do it.

Six years ago, my mentor challenged me not to quit on myself and fail through inaction—but to *try*. Facing threats to the future of our democracy, we can't afford to fail through inaction. We have to try.

IN THE FALL OF '17, I ARRIVED IN Charlottesville, Virginia, to perform at the University of Virginia's bicentennial celebration. It had been mere weeks since UVA was chosen as the site for a racist white nationalist rally. Images and video from the hate-filled, violent, tiki-torch march were everywhere—and a town and a university's reputation had been blighted collaterally. Twenty-two thousand alumni and longtime supporters were also scheduled to descend onto the campus in celebration.

There was no ignoring it once we arrived.

In a Q&A session with theater and other fine arts majors, a student raised her hand to jumpstart the afternoon. The first question of the day was, "In light of recent events here, Lil Yachty canceled a planned Charlottesville visit and concert. Future canceled his visit and his show. Why didn't *you*? Why didn't you cancel?"

The first question. What are you doing here?

"Well, I can leave if you want me to," I told her, "but I hope you'll let me stay for a bit."

She laughed. We all did.

But I knew what she was getting at.

I went on to tell her that there was no place I would rather be. "I wish I could've been here during the rally, too, to be honest."

Because we have been told for years that this type of hatred, this particular brand of divisiveness, *this* kind of sickness was a thing of the past in America—though we could *feel* otherwise. You want to believe it. You would be a fool to believe it.

The images coming out of Charlottesville told a different story.

Exit polls at the ballot box tell a *very* different story.

Woefully, it is the same old story, actually.

To stare down the rotting-flesh walking-dead Jim Crow zombies of yore—and even the undead lurching worm-fed corpses of Nazi Germany—with clear eyes, is to be woke in post-post-racial America.

"I wanted to see it all for myself," I told her.

So I wouldn't forget anything.

"And I wanted to see if I could help."

All true.

"Is that cool with you?" I asked.

"It is." She laughed and took her seat.

I'VE TRULY NEVER SEEN A COMMUNITY WORK so hard at meticulously and deliberately defining *themselves, for* themselves as I did at the two hundredth anniversary celebration for the University of Virginia.

With a unified voice, they took great care to say to the perpetuators of hatred, "You do not get to define us. That is not who we are."

And you know what, I believed 'em.

It's a reckoning once again for America. A Saturn Return.

What are we going to shout in our loud and unified voice?

Transition is an opportunity.

Let's take the opportunity.

Seriously.

ACKNOWLEDGMENTS

**OTHING ABOUT WRITING THIS** book has been easy. When I was asked to write it, I imagined I would retreat to some cabin in the woods and return to civilization after a few months clutching my tome—black Moses.

I never made it to the cabin. This book was written in motion. I wrote *on* planes, while waiting *for* planes, and in cars to and from airports. I wrote in dressing rooms, *hotel* rooms, and hotel *lobbies*. Thought by thought, word by word—by any means necessary we made it to the finish line.

What urged me onward, past the self-doubt and the exhaustion, and into the energy reserve and private stock of perseverance stashed inside each one of us, was the thought, *If the book can help one person it will have been worth it.*

I held a vision of you. The single reader was my guiding force. You were inspiring me long before we met. Thank *you*!

Do me a favor, say this name out loud wherever you are: Mim (rhymes with *Kim*) Eichler (Ike-ler) Rivas (Reeve-us).

Dear Mim, it is my favorite prayer—saying someone's *name* when they come to mind.

I imagine there is a record somewhere *up* there or *out* there. It has been recorded—the number of times our name has oozed out or dribbled out or absentmindedly fallen out or shot out of people's lips when we come to mind.

When our friends and loved ones say our names, when total strangers do, when our enemies curse us, the feeling in their bodies affect the buoyancy, the temperature, the coloring of the prayers. It determines how far the prayers will go and how fast they get there.

My hope is that our new reader friends tip the balances for you, in multiples of hundreds (and then thousands and then hundreds of thousands!!) for years and years to come.

Thank you for your mentorship and guidance. You picked up where Mrs. Turner left off. You reacquainted me with my true voice. There is no greater gift. I will never forget it.

Kat Brzozowski, *Failing Up* has benefited from your impeccable taste and sharp eye in untold ways. Thank you for all your hard work and for your support when I needed it most. I am so grateful.

Jean Feiwel! Thank you for this opportunity and this platform to express ideas that mean so much to me. Thank you for your trust and for your generosity.

To the Feiwel friends, Mary Van Akin, Melissa Zar, Molly Ellis, Alexei Esikoff, Kim Waymer, Patrick Collins, Gene Vosough, Raphael Geroni, thank you for adding your polish and professionalism to *Failing Up*! We made something we believe in. Thank you for helping us take it to the world!

Mollie Glick, Kevin Lin, and my team at CAA, I am represented by absolute stars. Thank you for encouraging and supporting all the many ways I desire to be creative. You are all so thorough and deft in your work. I am not sure how you do it. Thank you for connecting the dots between me and Feiwel and Friends. It was Match.com-level perfection. You are amazing.

For my teachers, some mentioned in these pages and some not: My sweet Nicolette. No one has taught me more than you, my angel. Thank you for dreaming the dream with me. My parents, my baby sis, my grandmother and grandfather, Mrs. Turner, Stuart K Robinson, the Robinson family, Billy Porter, Wren Brown, Miss Maureen, my brother Joseph Abate, and my young Lucille—add the story of my life to the evidence of the mark you've made in your time on this planet. Thank you for all you've given. I endeavor every single day to do you proud.

To the single reader, I hope you have found something helpful among these pages. The truth is, I hope you have found many things. I hope you will tell me about it the next time we see one another out in the world.